Peace Action

Freeze demonstrators in New York City, June 1982 *(photo by Mel Rosenthal)*.

Peace Action demonstrators in Washington, DC, September 2005 *(photo by Barbara G. Beckmann)*.

Peace Action

Past, Present, and Future

Edited by
Glen Harold Stassen
and Lawrence S. Wittner

Paradigm Publishers
Boulder • London

Paradigm Publishers is committed to preserving our environment. This book was printed on recycled paper with 30% post-consumer waste content, saving approximately 9 trees and avoiding the creation of more than 3,900 gallons of wastewater, more than 430 pounds of solid waste, nearly 850 pounds of greenhouse gases, and more than 1500 kilowatt hours of electricity than if it had been printed on paper manufactured from all virgin fibers.

Published in the United States by Paradigm Publishers, 3360 Mitchell Lane, Suite E, Boulder, Colorado 80301 USA.

Paradigm Publishers is the trade name of Birkenkamp & Company, LLC, Dean Birkenkamp, President and Publisher.

Library of Congress Cataloging-in-Publication Data

Peace action : past, present, and future / edited by Glen Harold Stassen and Lawrence S. Wittner.
   p. cm.
  Includes bibliographical references and index.
  ISBN 978-1-59451-332-9 (hardcover : alk. paper) — ISBN 978-1-59451-333-6 (pbk. : alk. paper) 1. Peace Action (Organization) 2. Peace movements—United States—History. I. Stassen, Glen Harold, 1936– II. Wittner, Lawrence S.
  JZ5584.U6P43 2007
  303.6'6--dc22

2007010971

Printed and bound in the United States of America on acid-free paper that meets the standards of the American National Standard for Permanence of Paper for Printed Library Materials.

Designed and Typeset by Straight Creek Bookmakers.

11   10   09   08   07   1   2   3   4   5

To the Reverend William Sloane Coffin Jr., 1924–2006
longtime peace activist,
former pastor of Riverside Church,
first president of SANE/Freeze,
and mentor for thousands in the worldwide struggle for peace and justice.
Through his splendid example,
he has helped us to understand, as he once declared:
"Hope arouses a passion for the possible,"
and the possible includes a brighter future for all humanity.

William Sloane Coffin Jr., 1980s *(photo by Paul Tick).*

Contents

Preface

Peace Action, the largest grassroots peace group in the United States, turned 50 in 2007. This half-century of existence began with the birth of SANE in 1957 and picked up momentum with the establishment of the Nuclear Weapons Freeze Campaign in 1979. In the late 1980s, SANE and the Freeze merged, forming SANE/Freeze; a few years later, the new organization was renamed Peace Action. Like their successor, SANE and the Freeze were the largest peace groups of modern times, with substantial influence upon public opinion and public policy. Yet surprisingly little is known about Peace Action's important history, its current activities, and its plans for the future.

Did you know, for example, that Eleanor Roosevelt, Martin Luther King Jr., Albert Schweitzer, and Walter Reuther were among Peace Action's early supporters? That its founder and first co-chair, Norman Cousins, was commissioned by President Kennedy to lay the groundwork with the Soviet government for the world's first nuclear arms control agreement, the Partial Test Ban Treaty? That it played a key role in bringing the Vietnam War to an end during the 1970s, in preventing nuclear war during the 1980s, and in ending the Cold War during the 1990s? Indeed, it is hard to imagine arms control and disarmament agreements or the willingness of governments to draw back from their reckless military adventures over the past half-century without the crucial work of Peace Action.

And what better people are there to recount Peace Action's exciting history, to distill lessons from its past, and to outline plans for its future than the women and men who led it? Drawn from the time of its founding to the present, they constitute an impressive group of individuals—bright, creative, and unswerving in their commitment to peace. One of them, Homer Jack, a founder of SANE, died some years ago. But he left behind his memoirs, from which we have taken his account of that organization's early history. The other leaders have been gracious enough to write original essays for this book.

As you will see, these leaders provide us with crucial insights into citizen activism for a more peaceful world—insights that are not otherwise easily attained. Most members of the public and public officials, only intermittently aware of peace movement activity, can hardly be expected to draw the appropriate lessons from the 50 tumultuous years of Peace Action's existence. Even many peace activists are too caught up in their day-to-day efforts to reflect upon the meaning of the past. This book, however, gathers together the wisdom of the past and of the present and points to a focused vision for our future in a brief and lively account. We hope that readers will learn from the new perspectives that it provides, thereby helping to move the world away from destruction and war toward real security and peace.

Naturally, we are proud to serve as editors of this collection. As longtime supporters of Peace Action and members of its national board, we feel honored to put together this book and to dedicate it to the late William Sloane Coffin Jr., the much-beloved former president of SANE/Freeze. And it has also been an honor to work on these essays with such thoughtful and steadfast supporters of peace. Some day, when the world has finally left the blood-stained barbarism of war behind, it will look back and accord them the enormous gratitude they deserve.

But enough editorial talk! Here is the story of Peace Action—past, present, and future.

—*Glen Harold Stassen and Lawrence S. Wittner*

Foreword

U.S. Representative Barbara Lee

Believe it or not, when I was a child I did not want to be a member of Congress when I grew up. What motivated me was not so much a desire to be part of our political system as a desire to change it.

When I was a student at Mills College in Oakland, California, I was a young, single mother on public assistance. Like many young people today, I was not registered to vote, because I just didn't think "the system" could or would work for me. When I looked at the white men who were running for President in 1972—Nixon, Humphrey, Wallace, Muskie, McGovern—I thought: why bother? None of them cares about me. They aren't going to take on the real issues that matter to people like me.

One of my professors gave us an assignment to work on one of the presidential campaigns, and I told him, you're going to have to flunk me, because there is *no way* I am going to work for one of them. That's when I first heard about Shirley Chisholm. Here was the first black woman elected to Congress, and she was talking about ending the war in Vietnam, about poverty, about civil rights, about women's rights;

and she was running for president! So I said I've got to find out more about this woman.

I was president of the Black Student Union, and I invited U.S. Representative Chisholm to come and speak to us on campus, and I went up and asked her what I could do to help with her campaign. And she looked at me and said: "Well the first thing you must do, my dear, is register to vote." It sounds common sense enough, but it really was a revelation. It was a lesson that she drilled home for a whole generation of us: if you care about what happens in our country or in the world, you can't just sit back and let someone else make the decisions. If you don't like "the system," then you've got to work to change it.

In many ways, Peace Action represents the very thing that motivated me to join Shirley's campaign and get involved in politics in the first place—the desire, not simply to advocate for progressive policies, but to change the way the political system works by giving people a voice in the legislative process.

My first encounter with Peace Action (then SANE) was in the mid-1970s, when I went to work as an intern for a newly elected antiwar U.S. representative named Ron Dellums. I saw firsthand the importance of SANE and, later, the Nuclear Freeze and other peace groups, prodding and supporting a busy member of Congress—in his case, already committed to the cause.

A lot has changed over the years—including the merger between SANE and the Nuclear Freeze that led to the formation of Peace Action—but that basic principle remains unchanged. What impressed me about the organization then, as today, was that it was able to harness people's spirit and idealism and the incredible disgust with certain U.S. policies—whether with the war in Vietnam, nuclear proliferation, arms sales, Pentagon pork, or the war in Iraq—and channel it, not simply into acts of protest, but into effective action geared toward changing the way our government works by involving people in the process.

In my home state of California, Peace Action's organizers are out knocking on doors, making calls, and organizing events in communities across the state just about every night. I know, because my colleagues and I get a lot of mail from people those organizers have talked to. They play an important role in educating people about everything from the development of new nuclear weapons to policies on arms sales and human rights. They help people realize the power they have when they act collectively, and they make sure politicians understand that when it comes to issues of war and peace, they have to answer to an informed and organized electorate.

In Washington, D.C., Peace Action plays the critical role of bringing together congressional staff and representatives of progressive foreign policy organizations in order to plan and share information, so that we can be more strategic and work together more effectively. Peace Action staff meet directly with members of Congress and their staffs to talk about key peace issues and to collaborate on legislative strategy on issues like ending the occupation of Iraq, changing U.S. foreign policy toward cooperation and human rights, and ridding the world of nuclear weapons.

In addition to working with legislators, Peace Action influences public policy by effectively getting its message out, not only through the media, but also in mass protests, in town hall meetings, and on the Internet.

Peace Action is one of the few peace groups that not only talks to members of Congress but helps elect candidates who understand and care about peace issues. Through its Peace Voter campaign, it educates millions of voters in every election about where candidates stand on peace issues. Peace Action's candidate endorsements, its campaign contributions, and its election organizers help elect progressive members of Congress to join me on the Congressional Progressive Caucus, which I currently co-chair.

At a time when corporations have more access and influence over our government than the people it was designed to serve and represent, Americans need an advocate like Peace Action that understands the sometimes byzantine workings of our government and can put that understanding to use advancing policies that foster peace and human rights.

I believe that members of Congress should be hearing more from constituents and peace activists than from lobbyists for the weapons or oil industry, and Peace Action is a model organization when it comes to making that happen. That is how we will achieve global security, peace, and justice.

It is an honor for me to contribute some thoughts for this book's foreword. I salute Peace Action's past work and I am proud to continue working with Peace Action in order to ensure a more peaceful future for our children and our grandchildren.

Chapter 1

A Short History of Peace Action

Lawrence S. Wittner

Peace Action grew out of the merger, in 1987, of two major U.S. peace organizations: the Committee for a Sane Nuclear Policy and the Nuclear Weapons Freeze Campaign.

SANE

The Committee for a Sane Nuclear Policy (better known as SANE) was founded in 1957, thanks to growing public concern about the nuclear arms race. Responding to an invitation by Norman Cousins (editor of the *Saturday Review*) and Clarence Pickett (secretary emeritus of the American Friends Service Committee), 27 prominent Americans met on June 21 in New York City's Overseas Press Club and launched an effort to focus American opinion on the dangers of nuclear testing. "The normal drive for survival has been put out of action by present propaganda,"

Norman Cousins, the founder and first co-chair of SANE *(records of SANE, Swarthmore College Peace Collection)*.

noted the eminent psychoanalyst Erich Fromm, and "we must ... try to bring the voice of sanity to the people." Accordingly, the group began to call itself the National Committee for a Sane Nuclear Policy.

SANE made its debut on November 15, 1957, with a dramatic advertisement in the *New York Times*. Signed by 48 well-known Americans, the ad argued that, although there existed more than enough nuclear weapons to destroy the human race, "our approach ... is unequal to the danger." They called for the immediate suspension of nuclear testing by all nations—an action that would halt radioactive contamination and provide "a place to begin on the larger question of armaments control." The "great challenge of the age," they declared, is to move beyond the traditional interests of the nation-state to "a higher loyalty"—loyalty to "the human community."

This advertisement unleashed a surge of antinuclear activity. Thousands of people responded—writing letters to SANE's tiny national office, republishing the advertisement in other newspapers, and holding local meetings. Thus, although SANE's founders had not planned to create a new organization, they soon had one on their hands. By the summer of 1958, SANE had 130 chapters and some 25,000 members, making it the largest peace group in the United States. Meanwhile, its leaders published new advertisements, held press conferences, distributed vast quantities of antinuclear literature, and gradually broadened SANE's goal to comprehensive nuclear disarmament.

In the following years, SANE became a very visible presence in American life. Hollywood SANE, organized by Steve Allen and Robert Ryan, mobilized a bevy of movie stars, including Tony Curtis, Janet Leigh, Anthony Quinn, Jack Lemmon, Shirley MacLaine, Gregory Peck, and Marlon Brando. In May 1960, SANE held an overflow rally at Madison Square Garden, with speeches by Eleanor Roosevelt and other luminaries.

Its newspaper ads were signed by influential world leaders such as Martin Luther King Jr., Albert Schweitzer, Bertrand Russell, Carlos Romulo, Gunnar Myrdal, and Trygve Lie. The best-known of SANE's ads featured the world's most famous pediatrician, Dr. Benjamin Spock, looking glumly down at a young child at play and proclaiming his grave concern at continued nuclear testing.

These ventures—and others by comparable movements in other nations—had a major impact upon nuclear weapons policies. Responding to the popular clamor, the U.S., British, and Soviet governments agreed in October 1958 to halt nuclear testing as they negotiated for a test ban

Eleanor Roosevelt, who signed SANE's first ads and was a featured speaker at its May 1960 Madison Square Garden rally, 1961 *(Franklin D. Roosevelt Library)*.

treaty. In addition, under the new administration of John F. Kennedy, the U.S. government built upon the institutionalization of arms control and disarmament that had begun during the Eisenhower administration to establish the Arms Control and Disarmament Agency.

Even after a breakdown of the testing moratorium in the fall of 1961, government officials remained impressed by the widespread public opposition to nuclear weapons tests. In late 1962, Kennedy met with Cousins of SANE and urged him to assure Soviet Premier Nikita Khrushchev of his sincerity in seeking a test ban treaty. Cousins began shuttling between the two world leaders and, in the spring of 1963, convinced Kennedy to deliver a speech that would signal a break with past hostility toward the Soviet Union. Delivered that June, this American University address—partially written by Cousins—emphasized the administration's desire to end nuclear testing and announced new test ban negotiations. This speech had a dramatic effect on Soviet leaders, thereby opening up the possibility for a thaw in the Cold War. That summer, U.S., British, and Soviet officials signed the Partial Test Ban Treaty, banning nuclear tests in the atmosphere, in outer space, and under water. Kennedy administration officials later emphasized the key roles played by SANE and Cousins in securing this first nuclear arms control treaty.

The Vietnam War and Its Aftermath

This early triumph, however, was followed by a difficult period for SANE, as it confronted the Vietnam War. SANE had been an early critic of U.S. military involvement in Vietnam, and in November 1965 organized the largest antiwar demonstration up to that time. For a time, SANE aligned itself with moderate peace groups by calling for a negotiated settlement of the conflict. But as the Johnson administration continued to spurn negotiations and to rely upon escalating military force, moderation became ever more difficult to sustain. In 1967, SANE's co-chair, Dr. Spock, headed up the Spring Mobilization to End the War in Vietnam, with a more militant agenda. SANE became the first nonpartisan group to oppose the reelection of President Lyndon Johnson and the first to support the peace candidacy of Sen. Eugene McCarthy, thereby helping to unleash a process that drove the president out of the Democratic party primaries and out of office. But the winner of the 1968 presidential race was Richard Nixon, who inspired no confidence whatsoever among peace activists. In December 1968, thoroughly disgusted with U.S. policy, SANE urged the withdrawal of U.S. troops from Vietnam.

In 1969, with the war grinding on under the Nixon administration, SANE played an active role in the 1969 Moratorium campaign and in the massive march on Washington to stop the war in Vietnam. Although SANE's top priority was ending the war, it did condemn the administration's development of an antiballistic missile system, a key element in the ongoing nuclear arms race. In 1972, it enthusiastically backed George McGovern's antiwar campaign for the presidency and, the following year, spearheaded congressional passage of the War Powers Act, which restricted presidential authority to initiate aggressive military action. Although Nixon easily won reelection, the war was doomed. As Henry Kissinger, his national security advisor and, later, secretary of state, recalled, the war and the peace protests "shattered the self-confidence" of U.S. officials. In 1975, when Congress refused to provide further military aid to the South Vietnamese government, the war ended.

In the aftermath of the Vietnam War, SANE swung back to highlighting the dangers of the arms race and, under the leadership of Seymour Melman, began to emphasize the need for economic conversion. In 1976, SANE secured an economic conversion plank in the campaign platform of the Democratic Party, and the Democratic candidate, Jimmy Carter, promised to do his utmost to implement it. The following year, SANE joined opponents of the B-1 bomber in successfully blocking the production and deployment of that weapon. Nevertheless, the post–Vietnam War era was hard on peace groups, which suffered from the public's sense of exhaustion. Some of them disappeared entirely. In 1976, SANE's membership fell to an all-time low of some 6,000.

SANE began to revive after October 1977, when David Cortright, who had been a leader of the GI antiwar movement, became its new executive director. With Soviet-American détente deteriorating, SANE focused upon backing the SALT II Treaty and, in 1978, economic conversion legislation, which—with support from major unions—was introduced in Congress by sympathetic legislators. One of the key unions was the International Association of Machinists, and, the following year, its president, William Winpisinger, became co-chair of SANE. Although SANE was pleased by the early policies of President Carter, it was alienated by his growing support for the military during the last years of his administration. In 1979, SANE launched a major campaign against the administration's MX missile program—mobilizing

President Jimmy Carter and Roslyn Carter march down Pennsylvania Avenue on inauguration day, as a SANE contingent reminds the new president of his professed goal of zero nuclear weapons, January 1977 *(records of Peace Action, Swarthmore College Peace Collection)*.

key groups and organizing against it in Western states. In 1980, SANE led a platform fight at the Democratic national convention against the missile program.

Beginning in 1981, the new Reagan administration's militarist agenda and loose talk of nuclear war sparked a vast upsurge of peace activism around the world, including the dramatic revival of SANE. By 1984, SANE's membership topped 100,000 Americans, and its weekly radio program, "Consider the Alternatives," carried on 140 stations, reached many more. Denouncing the Reagan administration's military priorities, SANE condemned plans for the deployment of new nuclear missiles in Europe and, in Congress, fought the administration to a near standstill over MX missiles. Although Reagan won reelection by a landslide in 1984, 106 of the 167 congressional candidates endorsed by SANE's political action committee emerged victorious.

The Nuclear Weapons Freeze Campaign

During the early 1980s, just as SANE became a major force in American politics, so did a new organization: the Nuclear Weapons Freeze Campaign. The Freeze arose in 1979 as the brainchild of Randy Forsberg, a young defense and disarmament researcher in Cambridge, Massachusetts. Recognizing that the clout of U.S. peace groups was limited by their organizational and programmatic division, she told a number of leading organizations that they would be far more effective if they united behind a proposal for a U.S.–Soviet agreement to halt the testing, production, and deployment of nuclear weapons. When they proved enthusiastic about her idea, she drafted the "Call to Halt the Nuclear Arms Race" in December 1979 and began circulating it among peace groups for feedback and endorsements. A Nuclear Freeze Steering Committee drew up a strategic plan for the period from 1980 to 1984. It called for lining up peace organizations, securing the backing of major interest groups, waging a major public education campaign to convert "middle America," and, finally, injecting the issue into mainstream politics. The campaign's potential was indicated in November 1980, when, prematurely, the Freeze was placed on the election ballot in western Massachusetts and, thanks to the efforts of Randy Kehler, Frances Crowe, and other local peace activists, it emerged victorious in 59 of the 62 towns voting on it.

Thereafter, the Freeze campaign made remarkable progress. Holding its first national conference in March 1981, it established a national headquarters in St. Louis, hired Kehler as its first national coordinator, and began organizing campaigns all across the country. In March 1982, 159 of 180 Vermont town meetings voted to back a U.S.-U.S.S.R. nuclear weapons freeze. On June 12 of that year, when peace groups sponsored an antinuclear demonstration in New York City around the theme of "Freeze the Arms Race—Fund Human Needs," it escalated into the biggest political demonstration in American history, with nearly a million participants. That fall, Freeze referenda appeared on the ballot in ten states, the District of Columbia, and 37 cities and counties. Although the Reagan administration worked zealously to defeat the referenda, in this largest referendum on a single issue in U.S. history (covering about a third of the U.S. electorate), over 60 percent of the voters supported the Freeze, leading to its victory in nine of the ten states and in all but three localities. Five different polls taken during 1983 found average support for the Freeze at 72 percent and opposition at 20 percent. Hundreds of national organizations, including major religious denominations and unions—many never involved before with national defense issues—endorsed the Freeze, as did more than 370 city councils and one or both houses of 23 state legislatures.

Stopping the Missiles, Ending the Cold War

This popular uprising had a major impact upon government officials. Recalling the Freeze campaign, Robert MacFarlane, Reagan's national security advisor, remarked years later: "We took it as a serious movement that could undermine congressional support for the [nuclear] modernization program, and ... a serious partisan political threat that could affect the election in '84." It necessitated what he called "a huge effort" to counter it, including extensive domestic and overseas speaking campaigns by Reagan and other government officials, mass media ventures, and administration denunciations of the Freeze campaign as initiated and controlled by the Kremlin. For the Democrats, it meant political opportunity. In May 1983, the Democratically controlled House of Representatives approved a Freeze resolution by a vote of nearly two to one. In 1984, the Freeze became part of the Democratic Party's official campaign platform. The Reaganites fought to get funding for the MX missile, but substantial opposition to it within Democratic ranks resulted in Congress's appropriating money for only 50 of the 200 missiles proposed.

Despite the Reagan administration's bitter opposition to peace groups, it was forced to modify its policies. In an effort to dampen popular protest against his nuclear buildup, the president endorsed the "zero option," a proposal—first advanced by the West German and Dutch governments under pressure from European peace organizations and the international representative of the Freeze campaign—to remove all intermediate-range nuclear missiles from Europe. Then he dropped plans to deploy the controversial neutron bomb. Then, in yet another concession to antinuclear sentiment, he agreed to abide by the provisions of the SALT II Treaty—although it had never been ratified and, during the 1980 campaign, he had attacked it as an act of "appeasement." In October 1983, in the midst of massive demonstrations against the deployment of U.S. cruise and Pershing II missiles in Western Europe, Reagan told his startled secretary of state: "If things get hotter and hotter and arms control remains an issue, maybe I should go see

[Soviet Premier Yuri] Andropov and propose eliminating all nuclear weapons." And, over the objections of his advisors, that's just what he did propose—beginning with a remarkable speech in January 1984.

Furthermore, in April 1982, shortly after the Freeze resolution was introduced in Congress, Reagan began declaring publicly that "a nuclear war cannot be won and must never be fought." He added: "To those who protest against nuclear war, I can only say: 'I'm with you!'" Against the backdrop of rising pressure against nuclear weapons, Reagan dramatically heightened his antinuclear rhetoric, telling the Japanese Diet in November 1983: "Our dream is to see the day when nuclear weapons will be banished from the face of the earth." He also began to press for a summit conference with Soviet leaders, which they resisted.

Reagan's turnabout occurred during his first term in office, and during his second he found a congenial partner in Mikhail Gorbachev. Taking office as Soviet party secretary in March 1985, Gorbachev was profoundly influenced by the worldwide antinuclear campaign. His "new thinking" about war and peace, Gorbachev declared, "took into account and absorbed the conclusions and demands of . . . the public . . . and of various antiwar organizations." The Soviet leader met frequently with antinuclear campaigners and, at international disarmament conferences, set aside time to confer with leaders of SANE and the Freeze.

In 1985, at the suggestion of antinuclear activists, Gorbachev began a unilateral moratorium on Soviet nuclear testing. In 1986, he helped craft an official Soviet blueprint for a nuclear-free world. In 1987, responding to advice from antinuclear activists, he took Reagan up on the president's offer of the zero option. Hard-line U.S. officials—who had viewed talk of the zero option as a propaganda gesture rather than as a serious negotiating proposal—were dismayed, but unable to resist. As Kenneth Adelman, Reagan's hawkish director of the Arms Control and Disarmament Agency, lamented, having proposed the zero option, "we had to take yes for an answer." The result was the signing later that year of the Intermediate Nuclear Forces Treaty, which eliminated all intermediate-range nuclear missiles from Europe. It was the first international agreement to scrap an entire class of nuclear weapons. These dramatic developments opened the way for further nuclear disarmament accords, as well as for an end to the Cold War.

For the Reaganites, it was a remarkable reversal. As Adelman recalled, unhappily: "Taking office considering Soviet behavior as the world's prime problem, Reagan came to consider nuclear weapons its main problem." Although "the administration assumed office practically brandishing nuclear weapons," its stance "metamorphosed ... into extreme antinuclear talk that resembled the nuclear bashers of SANE."

Nor could the new administration of George H.W. Bush escape the lingering influence of the movement. Bush and his secretary of state, James Baker, wanted to compensate for the scrapping of U.S. intermediate-range nuclear missiles by significantly upgrading U.S. short-range nuclear forces in Western Europe. But this plan grew exceptionally controversial after Gorbachev unilaterally removed Soviet short-range missiles from Eastern Europe. Baker recalled: "We were losing the battle for public opinion. We had to do something.... NATO could not afford another crisis over deploying nuclear weapons." As a result, the Bush administration retreated and agreed to negotiate missile reductions. Ultimately, it withdrew all short-range U.S. missiles from Western Europe and, in addition, signed the START I and START II treaties for significant reductions in long-range nuclear missiles.

Uniting SANE and the Freeze—Peace Action

Meanwhile, starting in the mid-1980s, pressure grew to unite SANE and the Freeze into one powerful organization. After all, they had much in common and, indeed, had worked closely together in the antinuclear campaign. Furthermore, in certain ways they were complementary, for SANE had a tightly knit national structure while the Freeze had a more fully developed grassroots presence. In addition, with Gorbachev and Reagan terminating the arms race and the Cold War, both groups experienced a loss of momentum, membership, funding, and coverage by the mass media. Consequently, in November 1987 they merged to form SANE/Freeze, an organization that activists hoped would provide the American peace movement with unprecedented power and influence. Headed by a new president, William Sloane Coffin Jr., SANE/Freeze had an estimated 200,000 members, chapters in every part of the United States, and an experienced, dedicated staff.

Thereafter, the new organization—renamed Peace Action in 1993—threw its efforts into halting the Department of Energy's nuclear weapons production, reducing military spending, slashing funding for the Reagan–Bush Star Wars program, convincing Congress to cut off funding for U.S.-backed wars in Central America, supporting sanctions against the apartheid regime in South Africa, and opposing U.S. military action in the Persian Gulf. On a more positive note, it worked at bettering relations with Gorbachev's Soviet Union, creating public support for a peace economy, and backing the Middle East peace process. In 1994, Rep. Cynthia McKinney and Sen. Mark Hatfield introduced legislation drawn up by Peace Action and other groups—the Arms Trade Code of Conduct—to block U.S. weapons sales to dictators and human rights abusers. In 1996, Peace Action initiated Peace Voter, a coordinated campaign of distributing millions of voter guides to Americans on the peace records of candidates for national public office.

The new organization's efforts to end nuclear testing proved particularly successful. In 1992—together with other peace groups—it helped steer legislation through the U.S. Congress that cut off funding for the only kind of U.S. nuclear tests permitted under the Partial Test Ban Treaty: those conducted underground. With U.S. nuclear testing now halted, the new president, Bill Clinton—under additional pressure from peace groups and their allies in Congress—negotiated the Comprehensive Test Ban Treaty. Speaking at the U.N. signing ceremonies in September 1996, U.S. Ambassador Madeleine Albright declared: "This was a treaty sought by ordinary people everywhere, and today the power of that universal wish could not be denied."

However, despite its political victories and the hopes of its founders, Peace Action—like most of the peace movement in the United States and abroad—was on the wane after the late 1980s and, particularly, after the end of the Cold War. By 1993, the organization's income had dropped substantially and its membership had fallen to about 50,000. Substantial cuts occurred in Peace Action's staff, and its influence ebbed. For the most part, this decline reflected a dwindling public perception of international crisis. Although the United States and the Soviet Union retained tens of thousands of nuclear weapons, the two countries were no longer poised to annihilate one another. Indeed, in late 1991, the Soviet Union ceased to exist.

Rising Militarism and a Reviving Peace Action

Even so, starting in the late 1990s, there were disturbing signs of renewed danger. These included, not only the eruption of many smaller wars, but India and Pakistan's development of nuclear weapons, the Republican-dominated U.S. Senate's resurrection of Star Wars and its rejection of the Comprehensive Test Ban Treaty, and the election in 2000 of George

W. Bush on a hawkish platform. Taking office, the Bush administration withdrew the United States from the ABM Treaty, began the deployment of a national missile defense system (a variant of Star Wars), blocked treaties to prevent the development and spread of chemical and biological weapons, refused to support the Comprehensive Test Ban Treaty and the treaty banning land mines, and plunged the U.S. government (plus any other governments it could corral) into a bloody invasion and military occupation of Iraq against the opposition of the United Nations. Meanwhile, it halted nuclear disarmament negotiations and pressed for the building of new nuclear weapons—despite the existence of some 30,000 of them (mostly in the arsenals of Russia and the United States), with thousands of these on hair-trigger alert.

Amid this rising militarism and unilateralism, Peace Action experienced a revival. Its membership grew dramatically, climbing to 100,000, while the Student Peace Action Network spread antiwar activism once more to the nation's campuses. In 2003, Peace Action launched the Campaign for a New Foreign Policy, mobilizing sympathetic organizations behind a program of supporting human rights and democracy, reducing the threat from weapons of mass destruction, and cooperating with the world community. Adding new staff members, Peace Action forged a close alliance with the Progressive Caucus in Congress, particularly in connection with ending the Iraq War, and also worked successfully to block the Bush administration's proposals for new nuclear weapons. In addition, Peace Action became an active participant in the two largest antiwar coalitions, United for Peace & Justice and Win Without War, thereby helping to turn out large numbers of people for vast antiwar demonstrations and for congressional lobbying days.

Thus, as Peace Action reached its 50th anniversary celebrations in 2007, it had not only survived the ebbs and flows of popular concern for peace, but had firmly established itself as the nation's largest peace organization, with deep roots in American life. Furthermore, although it had not brought an end to militarism, it had played an important role in halting numerous wars, fostering nuclear arms control and disarmament, and—overall—creating a saner, more humane world. No one, of course, knew exactly what the future would bring. But it was clear that, without the efforts of Peace Action, the planet would be a considerably more violent and dangerous place.

Chapter 2

The Beginnings of SANE

Homer A. Jack

On June 21, 1957, a cross section of American leaders met at the Overseas Press Club in New York City to discuss nuclear politics. The meeting grew out of many people's efforts, but one who stands out was Quaker peace activist Lawrence Scott of Chicago. In April he had convened a meeting of pacifists in Philadelphia to discuss the testing [of nuclear weapons] and proposed creating a Committee to Stop H-Bomb Tests. In the meantime they contacted Norman Cousins, editor of the *Saturday Review,* and Clarence Pickett of the American Friends Service Committee to give leadership. On May 29, Scott, Pickett, and myself met with Cousins in his office and decided to convene a meeting of individuals of national stature concerned with the end to nuclear testing. Pickett, who presided over the meeting of the Provisional Committee to Stop Nuclear Tests—later to be named SANE—suggested that "something should be done to bring out the latent sensitivity of the American people to the poisoning effect of nuclear bombs on international relations and humanity."

Lawrence Scott reported that non-pacifists all over the country were looking for national leadership to end testing. Poet Lenore G. Marshall (who met independently with Cousins and Pickett and later came to be viewed as a co-founder of the new organization) suggested arranging a meeting with President Eisenhower. Socialist leader Norman Thomas felt any ban on tests should be "but a first step to universal disarmament." Other participants included Earl Edwards of the American Friends Service Committee, Lawrence Mayers and John Swomley of the Fellowship of Reconciliation, Henry Hitt Crane, Rabbi Edward S. Klein, Harold Oram, Earl Osborn, Ralph Sockman, James Warburg, and Catholic Bishop (later Cardinal) John J. Wright. After five hours of discussion that first day of summer, the twenty-seven persons present appointed a smaller steering committee to take the next steps. In July the group established a clearinghouse for information on the cessation of nuclear tests. In the meantime, the group sent me to London to observe the negotiations of the U.N. Disarmament Subcommittee and then to Japan to evaluate the growing world movement to end nuclear testing.

A Committee Is Formed

On September 24, the full committee met again, also in New York. Cousins volunteered that he had recently visited Albert Schweitzer ... and found him "with low spirits—heartsick at what is happening in the world." Lenore Marshall urged the group to "think of projects on a much larger scale," such as gaining a court injunction against further American tests. Psychoanalyst Erich Fromm observed that the ... group must "try to bring the voice of sanity to the people."

Co-chairman Clarence Pickett reminded the group that it was not yet officially organized. He asked whether existing organizations could effectively stop nuclear tests, and the group responded that a new national organization was genuinely needed. These pioneers decided to hire an executive secretary and select a board of directors that could represent many interests and organizations.

By October the new organization had defined its broad purposes as preventing nuclear war and creating a global order of peace with justice.

Its first task was "the immediate cessation of nuclear weapons tests by all countries, including our own, through a U.N.-monitored program."

At a committee meeting on October 1, Cousins suggested placing a prominent advertisement to "define the issue in its purest form and provide the people with an action program." On November 15, 1957, the *New York Times* carried a full-page advertisement with the headline: "We Are Facing a Danger Unlike Any Danger That Has Ever Existed." The text called upon all nations to suspend nuclear weapons tests. Published shortly after the launching of Sputnik, the advertisement declared that "the test of a nation's right to survive today is measured not by the size of its bombs or the range of its missiles, but by the size and range of its concern for the human community as a whole."

The copy was largely Norman Cousins' work, and the ad was endorsed by a diverse group of American intellectuals, including Cleveland Amory, John C. Bennett, Harrison Brown, Harry Emerson Fosdick, Oscar Hammerstein II, John Hersey, Stanley Livingston, Lewis Mumford, Eleanor Roosevelt, Howard Thurman, and Paul Tillich. The advertisement soon appeared in twenty-three U.S. newspapers, reaching a total circulation of more than 3 million, including the *Washington Post,* the *Chicago Sun-Times,* and the *Los Angeles Times.* National SANE received 2,300 responses from thirty-six states and more than $12,000 in donations.... Almost overnight the ads created SANE groups in fifteen major cities and informal ones in forty-one others.

Joining SANE

I served as Executive Director of SANE from October 15, 1960, through September 15, 1964.... When people asked me why I went to work for SANE, I would say glibly that "Norman Cousins wanted me to get SANE from out of the shadow of dealing with Senator Dodd." (Dodd was accusing SANE of being communist-influenced.) Yet in reviewing the archives of SANE ,... I realize that was indeed an idealized answer. SANE was in deep trouble that summer of 1960, facing a crisis of confidence and finances.... Both Cousins and Pickett wanted to be relieved of their chairmanship.... The debt was $9,000, with a balance in the bank of $174.71.... Cousins and others on the SANE Board convinced me that I must come to "save SANE."

SANE was only three years old when I became director. It had two previous directors for brief periods: Trevor Thomas and Donald Keys. I felt my first task was administrative. In place was an excellent staff: Sanford Gottlieb, a former newspaperman and labor official, living in Washington; Donald Keys, one of SANE's founders and a world federalist; and Edward Meyerding. I knew Ed from Chicago, where he was director of the Illinois chapter of the American Civil Liberties Union, of which I was vice-chairman....

We assigned staff responsibilities in our little office at 17 East 45th Street, only one block from Cousins' office at the *Saturday Review*. Gottlieb handled dealing with the Administration and Congress as political director. Keys dealt with [the] program. Meyerding dealt with finances and fund-raising. I assumed other responsibilities, including dealing with both the board and the chapters, working at the U.N., and relating to overseas test-ban and disarmament organizations. We held frequent staff meetings and made written reports to the board, often every two months. I emphasized communications and in 1961 we changed over our periodical, *SANE U.S.A.,* to *SANE World*—which lasted into the 1980s.... We became a good team, despite a low budget. We began to evolve an enlightened employee policy and, in time, welcomed unionization.

One of my most pleasant tasks was to help relate SANE to the U.N. system. Our office was only 15 minutes' walk to U.N. Headquarters. We soon obtained U.N. credentials, despite their preferring to deal with international non-governmental organizations. Thus we became an NGO....

I soon found that the First or Disarmament Committee of the General Assembly, meeting every October and November, was a splendid place to meet the disarmament ambassadors of the principal countries testing nuclear weapons: U.S.S.R., U.K., and U.S.A.—and later France and China. While the disarmament secretariat of the U.N. was located in New York, it also became apparent that any significant test-ban negotiations—bilateral or multilateral—would take place at Geneva.

Despite the costs, we occasionally flew to Geneva to obtain political information on the course of the negotiations, news we could not obtain in New York or Washington. In 1961 the McCloy-Zorin [disarmament] negotiations took place in New York.... We were elated with what we heard, for the next step appeared to involve new negotiations for a test-ban.

In March 1962, the Eighteen-Nation Disarmament Conference ... started to meet. SANE collected a useful array of disarmament books and gave this library to each of the eighteen diplomatic missions. Each contained a SANE bookmark. They were appreciated and some of the volumes were in use, or at least available, in some diplomatic missions in Geneva more than two decades afterwards!

I had known some of the U.S. delegates in Washington and New York, and I talked with them ... [in a more] leisurely [way] at their offices in the U.S. Disarmament Mission at Geneva. I also met the principals of other key delegations, especially the Soviet Union, Sweden, France, the U.K., India, and Japan.

Public Education Campaign

In the campaign against nuclear testing and on behalf of peace initiatives, SANE made increasing use of the mass media—especially full-page advertisements—to educate the public on the issues and pressure national and world leaders. Doyle, Dane and Bernbach, our advertising agency, was one of the most creative at the time.... They contributed their services in our continuing series of full-page advertisements. (We still had to pay the newspapers for space!) Between 1957 and 1964, we ran over thirty ads focusing attention on the issues. Banner headlines proclaimed:

"No Contamination Without Representation"

"Nuclear Bombs Can Destroy All Life"

"Of Candidates and Cranberries"

"An Open Letter to President Kennedy"

"Berlin: There Is an Alternative"

"Soviet Nuclear Tests, a Crime"

"Is This What It's Coming To?" (with the picture of a contaminated milk bottle)

"Mr. President, Help Us to Get Behind You"

"The Next Time Madness Strikes"

"Nuclear Tests Must End"

As world public opinion turned against testing, the U.S. and U.S.S.R. observed an unofficial moratorium.... Following the Berlin Crisis and resumption of nuclear tests in 1961, however, SANE went back on the offensive. "It is never too late," we declared, "nor too unpatriotic to tell the President that he should postpone atmospheric tests until a test-ban treaty can be negotiated in Geneva." We organized student conferences and convened panels of scientists and other experts to voice their opposition. We called on the American people to bombard the President with letters, telegrams, and calls for an end to atomic and hydrogen weapons testing. In early February 1962, the heaviest mail on any single issue during the whole Kennedy Administration was received at the White House. Western Union called it "a flood," and the tide of telegrams against testing remained at the top of the list of citizens' concerns for sixteen weeks.

Dr. Spock Is Worried

SANE was always looking for new, visible personalities to add to our National Board or our National or International Advisory Committees. We did well and our National Board included such members of the cultural elite ... as writer and psychoanalyst Erich Fromm, actor Robert Ryan, and TV personality Steve Allen. Our National and International Advisory Boards contained Bertrand Russell, Albert Schweitzer, Pablo Casals, Martin Luther King Jr., and Harry Belafonte. We could always add new names and several persons suggested that we invite the Cleveland pediatrician, Benjamin Spock, author of the best-selling *Baby and Child Care*.

In 1960 someone at SANE approached Dr. Spock. His biographer Lynn Z. Bloom, reproduced his original letter of refusal: "I am in agreement with [your] policy.... I have no expert knowledge at all about the relationship between radiation and health. If I were to take any official part in the work of the Committee I think that many parents would assume 1) that I was, to some degree, an expert and 2) that as an expert I was alarmed by the present dangers of radiation. To put it another way: I have tried as parent educator to be non-alarmist, and I want to save my influence to use in areas in which I feel I have competence.... I feel ashamed to turn you down, but I have to. I hope you ... forgive me."

We did forgive him and did not pursue him at that time. However, on January 15, 1962, I wrote Spock ... inquiring again whether he might become a national sponsor of SANE. I explained our mission in one sentence: "We were established in 1957 and have tried ever since to

SANE's famous "Dr. Spock Is Worried" ad, run in the April 16, 1962, issue of the *New York Times* (records of SANE, *Swarthmore College Peace Collection*).

lead American public opinion in favor of an inspected ban on nuclear weapons tests and substantial steps toward disarmament." I enclosed some materials. I suggested that the "duties of a national sponsor are minimal, but you would be kept informed of the policies and program of the National Committee and will be consulted occasionally on special problems." I ended by indicating that "we would cherish your cooperation by becoming a national sponsor," pointing out the long column on the letterhead of "the company you would be keeping."

Two days later, Spock responded to my letter: "I appreciate being invited to be a sponsor of SANE.... I am much in favor of what SANE is doing. But I do not wish to be listed because I think that some anxious parents will assume that as a physician I have expert knowledge on radiation and that I am alarmed about present levels from fallout."

This time I did not forgive Spock.... How could I change his mind? Suddenly I realized that Albert Einstein faced the same dilemma that Spock faced. After Einstein received the Nobel Prize in physics in 1921, he asked himself: should I use my new fame only in my field of physics or should I transfer it to my deep concern for human affairs? I remember preaching about Einstein's dilemma in a sermon I delivered when I was minister of the Unitarian Church in Evanston [Illinois] in the 1950s.

I looked up that old sermon and found I had quoted Philipp Frank in his biography of Einstein:

> Einstein realized that the great fame that he had acquired placed a great responsibility upon him. He considered that it would be egotistic and conceited if he simply accepted the fact of his recognition and continued to work on his researches.
>
> He saw that the world was full of suffering and he thought he knew some causes. He also saw that there were many people who pointed out these causes, but were not heeded because they were not prominent figures. Einstein realized that he himself was now a person to whom the world listened, and consequently he felt it his duty to call attention to those sore spots and so help eradicate them.
>
> ... He knew no more about such things than any other educated person. The advantage he possessed was that he could command public attention and he was a man who was not afraid, if necessary, to stake his reputation....

In a week ... I replied to Spock's refusal. I began: "I must accept your opinion not to become a sponsor of SANE, but your reasons sent me to my books on Albert Einstein." Then I gave that long quotation....

I ended my letter to Spock ... : "If I may say so, I think there are some parallels here in your case. SANE is not primarily an anti-fallout organization. Our central theme is controlled and comprehensive disarmament, although we are concerned about fallout if atmospheric tests continue. But we desperately want and need leaders such as yourself 'to whom the world listens.'"

... Within a month, and I am sure due to influences beyond my letter (including a speech by President Kennedy trying to defend his resumption of tests), Spock wrote me ... : "As a result of a number of factors including your letter and the drift of events I have changed my mind and am ready to be listed as a sponsor of SANE."

... On April 16—barely six weeks after Spock came aboard—the [next SANE] full-page advertisement appeared in the *New York Times*. Most of the page was devoted to a picture of Dr. Spock—dressed in a business suit—with a child. The heading of the page read: "Dr. Spock Is Worried." Then followed seven short paragraphs, boiled down from 4,000 words which Spock carefully wrote....

This was the most successful public education ad SANE ever inserted. It cost $5,000 and soon reappeared in eighty papers and magazines around the world, all paid for by local SANE and other peace groups. Thousands of copies of the advertisement were reproduced and circulated.

By June, the public was so wrought up over nuclear testing and its potential harm to individual and family health, especially that of children, that columnist Drew Pearson wrote that President Kennedy's resumption of testing was the most unpopular thing he had ever done, "The nuclear letters are running about four to one against the President." It took another year for the test-ban treaty to be concluded. But Dr. Spock's public appeal ... must be regarded as a turning point in awakening the conscience of the world to the effects of nuclear testing and the imperative of ending the arms race.

Other Aftereffects

After the April ad appeared, SANE was identified with Spock and Spock with SANE.... Within a year ... he became co-chair of the organization with H. Stuart Hughes, a professor of history at Harvard University.

Norman Cousins by then was increasingly working with the Kennedy Administration on the test-ban treaty.... I watched with fascination as he acted as courier among President John F. Kennedy, Secretary

Khrushchev, and Pope John XXIII. While relaying messages between Washington and Moscow, Cousins told the President that strontium-90 had been found in milk all over the world after the last round of Soviet and American tests and that the people wanted an end to nuclear testing. In the Soviet Union, he showed Khrushchev a copy of SANE's advertisement proclaiming "We Can Kill the Russians 360 Times Over ... The Russians Can Kill Us Only 160 Times Over ... We're Ahead, Aren't We?"

... By the time I left the staff of SANE in September 1964, the test-ban treaty was signed, ratified, and entered into force.

Source for this chapter: Homer A. Jack, with editing by Alex Jack, *Homer's Odyssey: My Quest for Peace and Justice* (Becket, MA: One Peaceful World Press, 1996), pp. 267–276. Used with permission.

Chapter 3

SANE's Early Years

Sanford Gottlieb

At the birth of SANE in November 1957, the U.S. political climate was dominated by fear and distrust, spawned by the Cold War. The spirit of McCarthyism still lived. Americans felt threatened by Communism and expected a war with the Soviet Union.

Testing and development of H–bombs by both sides added to the fears of cataclysmic conflict and also raised more immediate fears: a new threat to human health. The Eisenhower administration, determined to preserve nuclear arms as the mainstay of national security, hid the dangers of nuclear fallout. Later we learned from scientists not on the government payroll that cows eat grass contaminated by radioactive fallout and pass along strontium–90 in their milk to children and adults.

In that political climate and with officialdom treating dissenters as traitors or dupes, the first full-page SANE ad in the *New York Times* broke like a sunburst in a storm. Sponsored by a group of distinguished Americans, including Eleanor Roosevelt, the ad was written largely by

Norman Cousins, editor of the *Saturday Review*. It called for an end to nuclear testing and the arms race and stressed our allegiance to "the human community." Along with a few thousand other citizens, I clipped the coupon from the ad and sent a small donation to the National Committee for a Sane Nuclear Policy at a post office box in New York.

The sponsors of the ad, who shared the naive assumption that a series of eloquent ads could change U.S. policy, did not intend to launch a membership organization. Nonetheless, the response from the grassroots impelled the sponsors in New York to do just that.

The organization soon became known as SANE, with Unitarian minister Homer Jack as executive director. Local chapters sprang up and in time received one-third of the seats on the New York-based board of directors. The initial top leadership came from pacifists and the United World Federalists. Most of the 25,000 people who eventually joined, however, were drawn in good part from the World War II generation and were neither pacifists nor world federalists. They were united in opposing the Bomb.

Although 25,000 members make up a tiny percentage of a big country's population, the fledgling organization's dynamism raised public consciousness and had an impact on government policy. Additional ads, written and illustrated pro bono by one of the top Madison Avenue advertising firms, appeared in the *New York Times* and other newspapers and evoked an enthusiastic response. Speakers fanned out to church basements, house meetings, and outdoor rallies. Activists distributed literature wherever crowds gathered. Some marched with banners calling for a nuclear test ban. Others wrote letters and lobbied members of Congress. Hollywood for SANE was organized, with entertainer Steve Allen and actor Robert Ryan speaking to numerous groups in the Los Angeles area and beyond. Later, Labor for SANE forged the first alliance with progressive trade unionists. Guided by Seymour Melman, professor of industrial engineering at Columbia University, SANE became the first organized voice to urge the conversion of the arms industry to nonmilitary pursuits.

Strong Enough to Arouse an Opposition

Not everyone was enthralled at this collective surge of energy. The New York *Daily News* called SANE's leaders "as nutty as so many fruitcakes." *Time* magazine was more insidious in 1958. It asserted that the members' activity "was what the sworn enemies of religion, liberty and peace itself were telling them to do." In short, we were typecast as pawns of the Communist conspiracy.

There were other obstacles. One was the lack of prominent authority figures at the grassroots to carry SANE's message and persuade the skeptics. Another hurdle came from the undeniable fact that much of what we talked about generated fear. On the one hand, rational fear of radioactive fallout and of nuclear war had created SANE; on the other hand, the public can absorb only limited talk of impending doom. So where to draw the line? Did the SANE ad showing a cockroach (highly resistant to radiation) and headlined "The winner of World War III" cross that line? The ad showing a pregnant woman and captioned "1 and 1/4 million unborn children will be born dead or have some gross defect because of nuclear bomb testing" apparently did not. It was enormously popular, was reproduced as a poster, and appeared on hundreds of New York City subway trains and platforms.

When the United States Information Agency opened a graphic arts exhibit in Moscow in 1963, Soviet visitors looked around and asked, "Where are the peace posters?" The USIA urgently contacted SANE. The pregnant-woman poster and others were rushed to Moscow. The graphic artists who designed posters for SANE were among the many unsung heroes of this period. Among their most effective ones were black-and-white posters portraying President Kennedy, Pope Pius XII, and General Omar Bradley with their statements on war and peace. I remember a Maryland Labor Day parade where fellow SANE members and I carried those posters—and got applauded! That didn't happen every day.

Getting Serious about Getting Organized

SANE opened a Washington office in 1960 and hired me as political action director. A new round of activities began: more focused lobbying advice for grassroots members; a search for friends on Capitol Hill; occasional testimony before relevant congressional committees and the platform committees of both parties; and working in coalition with like-minded religious and peace groups. With them, SANE helped organize the 1960 Campaign for Disarmament, which distributed the (very limited) statements on disarmament by the major candidates for president. When the Republicans held platform hearings that year, I accompanied Steve Allen to make SANE's pitch for a test ban treaty. Steve settled himself comfortably in the witness chair and began, "I'm here representing an interest group known as the human race." But his testimony didn't make a dent in the GOP's hawkish platform.

Congressional committees were no friendlier. SANE couldn't trot out any retired generals or former secretaries of state to impress them, and the House Armed Services Committee (HASC) for years wouldn't even allow nongovernmental witnesses to testify. When HASC finally opened its doors and an opportunity presented itself, I tried a different tack. Testifying before the hardest-line committee in Congress, I completely avoided mention of nuclear weapons. Instead, I listed all of the worldwide military commitments made by the executive branch, many without approval by Congress. The total was over 40. The HASC members apparently hadn't heard this before. They reacted with irritation, not with me but with the executive branch that had bypassed them. Rep. Otis Pike, a prickly Long Island Democrat, remarked that he'd have to change his mind about SANE. In that context, it was warm praise. Other members expressed similar comments. The *Washington Post* wrote a feature about this unusual exchange.

An Effort to Weaken Our Increasingly Effective Efforts

Another member of Congress, Sen. Tom Dodd (D-CT), was less sympathetic. As a SANE rally hailing the planned summit of President Eisenhower and Premier Khrushchev was about to begin at Madison Square Garden in May 1960, New York *Journal-American* headlines screamed that Dodd was charging Communist infiltration of New York SANE.

For months a thorny issue had been debated within the SANE board. Two of the organization's leaders, Norman Thomas and the Reverend Donald Harrington, had reported that some activists in the New York area appeared unable or unwilling to criticize actions of the Soviet government but had no qualms about criticizing the U.S. government. Thomas and others tried repeatedly to formulate a policy that would address this tilt. Others on the board, however, objected that a policy aimed at screening out Communists would be a violation of civil liberties. No action was taken.

Dodd, the temporary chairman of the Senate Internal Security Subcommittee, subpoenaed 28 New York SANE members. After much internal turmoil, SANE's board finally adopted the following policy:

"Members of the Communist Party, fascists or individuals who are not free because of party discipline or political allegiance to apply to the actions of the Soviet Union and the Chinese government the same standards by which they challenge others are not welcome on any level of this organization." In the stormy aftermath, several board members resigned and some local chapters dissolved.

Meanwhile, the summit meeting that was the focus of the Garden rally had collapsed when a U-2 spy plane was downed over the U.S.S.R. and Khrushchev walked out. Yet, the rally had been memorable. Eleanor Roosevelt, former GOP presidential candidate Alf Landon, Walter Reuther of the United Auto Workers, civil rights leader A. Philip Randolph, Michigan Governor G. Mennen Williams, and Cousins and Thomas addressed a packed house. Harry Belafonte performed. After the rally, Reuther, Thomas, and Belafonte led a march of 5,000 persons to the United Nations for a prayer vigil.

Pressing the Kennedy Administration

The Kennedy administration brought new possibilities. Kennedy was cautious but open. His science adviser, Jerome Wiesner, favored nuclear restraint, but other top officials were still in the grip of Cold War thinking. While the administration was considering a civil defense plan, which SANE believed would trigger panic, I visited Adam Yarmolinsky in the Pentagon. He was one of Robert McNamara's "whiz kids." SANE had asked its members to write to him and other newly appointed officials in support of disarmament measures. "You have a lot of members in California," Yarmolinsky observed. Apparently the Californians had been our most prolific letter-writers. I told Yarmolinsky that testimony before the Joint Atomic Energy Committee indicated a nuclear attack above a certain level (10,000 megatons) would render fallout shelters completely useless. Yarmolinsky looked pained.

Calling in an aide, he repeated what I had said. Turning to the only thing on his huge desk, a copy of Herman Kahn's *On Thermonuclear War,* Yarmolinsky patted the book and, in a whiny voice, complained, "That can't be true, can it? Because if it's true, Herman is wrong!" Herman Kahn, strategist of the unthinkable, wrote that tome to make nuclear war seem both acceptable and winnable.

The Kennedy administration's flirtation with civil defense continued for a while. SANE learned that a decision was pending on whether to send every American household a brochure promoting installation of fallout shelters. Teaming up with the Reverend Rodney Shaw of the Methodist Division of World Peace, we activated two telephone chains to reach our respective activists across the country. We asked them to send telegrams to the White House with this message: If you distribute the fallout-shelter brochures, we will organize a campaign to send them back. The brochure was never mailed. Eventually, particularly after Southern politicians began inquiring whether public shelters would be segregated, the civil defense plan evaporated.

When Kennedy sent Cuban exiles to invade Castro's Cuba at the Bay of Pigs, SANE members were furious. They wanted to come to Washington to protest to a top official. I requested an appointment with McGeorge Bundy, the national security adviser. He rejected meeting with a delegation but agreed to meet with me. Careful to be punctual, I waited while he met with the Joint Chiefs of Staff. When the chiefs exited, his secretary ushered me in. Bundy sat at his desk signing letters. He didn't look up, didn't greet me, didn't ask me to sit down. So I stood and said my piece, namely that we ignore other peoples' nationalism at our peril and that nationalism shouldn't be confused with Communism. Bundy uttered his first, and only, words: "There's much force in what you say." That ended the meeting.

One victory came about even as bigger Cold War crises loomed. President Kennedy signed the bill, advocated by SANE and the United World Federalists, creating the Arms Control and Disarmament Agency in 1961. ACDA, reporting to both the president and the secretary of state, provided institutional clout to arms controllers inside the government. Without ACDA, says ex-arms negotiator Lawrence Weiler, the nuclear Non-Proliferation Treaty might never have been negotiated.

In 1961, when the Soviets triggered the Berlin Crisis, SANE published ads in 12 newspapers calling for a four-power Berlin authority and, ultimately, a disarmed Germany. The superpowers had other ideas; both ended temporary moratoriums on nuclear testing. Then the U.S.S.R. placed nuclear missiles in Cuba and the world came close to nuclear war. SANE and many others issued appeals for restraint, but we all felt quite powerless. Toward the end of the Cuban Missile Crisis, Homer Jack and I met with Arthur Schlesinger Jr., Kennedy's assistant, at the White House. He assured us the crisis was being resolved.

The close call sobered the superpower leaders. Kennedy had already shown his positive side in a speech to the U.N. a month before the missile crisis. He challenged the Soviets to a "peace race" instead of

SANE leaders and allies at SANE's November 27, 1965, rally for peace in Vietnam are (left to right): Norman Thomas, Dr. Spock, Sanford Gottlieb, Barbara Dane (folksinger), and Edwin Dahlberg (former president, National Council of Churches). At the upper right are Homer Jack, chatting with Carl Oglesby (chair of Students for a Democratic Society) *(Sanford Gottlieb).*

an arms race, adopting the phrase coined earlier by Seymour Melman, and developed into a policy statement by SANE. "Mankind must put an end to war," Kennedy added. The president then made a dramatic commitment to world disarmament. By early 1963, a test ban treaty seemed the logical next step.

First, some of the underbrush of distrust had to be cleared away. Norman Cousins played a major role in conveying back-channel messages between Kennedy and Khrushchev. He also contributed much of the text for Kennedy's speech at American University, a breakthrough call for an end to the Cold War that set the tone for an accord. The Limited Test Ban Treaty that resulted, after years of negotiation, halted atmospheric tests and prohibited tests under the sea or in outer space, but permitted underground tests to continue. With Kennedy's help, Cousins organized a citizens committee to rally support for ratification, which came on a Senate vote of 80 to 19.

The treaty was an environmental and political success, but nuclear arms development continued. There was also an organizational downside: With fears of fallout ended, SANE and like-minded groups lost members. Nonetheless, SANE's work expanded.

Pressing Lyndon Johnson

SANE went on to oppose the Vietnam War, the anti-ballistic missile system, B-1 bomber, MX missile, and excessive military spending. In 1969 SANE published the most successful cause ad in history: "From the people who brought you Vietnam: The anti-ballistic missile system." Edward Sorel's satirical drawing of Pentagon brass adoring a missile mock-up touched a nerve. The *Wall Street Journal* and *Time* used the ad to illustrate articles, and 5,000 poster reproductions were hung in college dorms, homes, and even congressional offices.

SANE outlined a strategy for demilitarizing American society, proposed legislation for conversion of the arms industry, and tried to build coalitions based on common interests in allocation of the federal tax dollar. As part of its outreach program, SANE invited the Italian-American political leader in Newark, Steven Adubato, to address its 1971 national conference. Adubato urged liberals to respect the symbols of working-class ethnics, especially the American flag. He described SANE's flag-adorned bumper sticker—"Honor America, Leave Vietnam"—as "brilliant, whether you know it or not." Privately Adubato told me, "That bumper sticker was the first one I could use in my neighborhood without getting stoned."

SANE was a pioneer in peace politics. The impetus came in 1962 from Los Angeles, where members of SANE and Women Strike for Peace provided 300 volunteers for three congressional candidates who agreed to support a nuclear test ban and oppose civil defense. Two, George Brown Jr., and Edward Roybal, were elected. For decades they were stalwarts of the pro-arms control minority in the House. Following the Los Angeles initiative, SANE created a procedure for the joint endorsement of congressional candidates by local chapters and the national board, but it was used infrequently. The peace movement was slow to recognize that policy change is rarely achieved by pressure groups alone. Influence in a major political party is also necessary.

That insight came during the Vietnam War, for SANE members if not for others. By 1967, SANE's advocacy of peace politics led to its major role in the "Dump Johnson" movement. In January 1968, SANE became the first nonpartisan organization to endorse Eugene McCarthy for president. SANE activists flocked to the McCarthy campaign and worked vigorously for a peace plank at the Democratic convention, but the odds were against them. In 1971, SANE called for local efforts to generate pressure on specific members of Congress and elect alternative candidates to Congress and the presidency. When a resolution supporting that targeted approach was submitted to an antiwar convention sponsored by the National Peace Action Coalition, however, it received only eight votes from the nearly 1,000 delegates. For movement radicals, politics was still a dirty word—even if preceded by the word "peace."

Peace Makes Good Politics

Looking back, Arthur Schlesinger Jr., remarked years later: "The Kennedy administration welcomed pressure from domestic arms control groups as an offset against the pro-arms-race pressure from Congress and the military." Sadly, Kennedy was slow to recognize that peace made good politics. He went on a Western speaking tour while the test ban treaty was awaiting ratification by the Senate and was pleasantly surprised by the warm applause that greeted his brief mention of the treaty. A few months later he was dead.

Politicians rarely understand the advantage of having others out ahead of them, breaking ground with new ideas. Sen. George McGovern was breaking ground in 1963 when he introduced an amendment to cut $5 billion from the $53.6 billion "overkill" defense budget. He noted, "Today, the two superpowers ... have piled up nuclear weapons with an explosive power of 60 billion tons of TNT—enough to put a 20-ton bomb on the head of every human being on the planet." I ran into McGovern on his way to deliver that speech. We were stopped in the Senate corridor by Hubert Humphrey, then majority whip. "I've read that speech of yours, George," Humphrey said, "and it's a helluva great one, but are you sure you want to give it now? It might scare the opponents of the test ban treaty." McGovern gave his speech. His amendment failed, but his reputation rose. The treaty was ratified. And SANE endorsed McGovern for president in 1972.

In a Cold War environment, SANE provided a political space for dissenters. Seeking to end the dangerous arms race, it helped educate a fearful public and pressure a military-minded government. With allied groups in Europe and Japan, the growing American peace movement persuaded the superpowers to accept temporary halts to nuclear testing,

U.S. Senator George McGovern receives SANE's Eleanor Roosevelt Peace Award at a SANE award dinner, November 9, 1965 *(records of SANE, Swarthmore College Peace Collection)*.

and then to sign the Limited Test Ban Treaty. But when the emotion-laden issue of fallout disappeared, the movement declined. This pattern recurred during the Vietnam War when the draft ended and Nixon started bringing troops home, and in the Reagan years when officials halted their bellicose rhetoric and Reagan discovered the value of negotiating. The challenge for peace groups, then and now, is to connect strongly felt current issues with long-term practical goals—and recruit members who are ready for the long haul.

Chapter 4

The Vietnam War and SANE's Change of Focus

Marcus Raskin

In the waning days of the Eisenhower period, there seemed a real possibility of turning off the war engine. In his historic 1960 farewell address, President Dwight Eisenhower warned against the military–industrial complex, which he maintained would change the character of the United States and endanger the world. This warning gave hope and support to disparate thinkers and activists connected to SANE, such as A.J. Muste, Clarence Pickett, and Norman Cousins, and included Linus Pauling and those scientists who supported the *Bulletin of the Atomic Scientists*. Here was President Eisenhower sounding the alarm, claiming that the national security policies of the United States put republican government in mortal danger. Eisenhower had said that thermonuclear war was unthinkable, and yet planners in Moscow and Washington had plans for this "eventuality" with its horrifying implications. It was no wonder that the peace movement and especially SANE were looked to at the end of the 1950s and the beginning of the 1960s for a moral authority.

Some personal history may be of use in understanding my own vantage point on these matters. Before joining the special staff of the National Security Council (NSC), I worked for a number of Democratic members of Congress, notably Robert Kastenmeier and James Roosevelt. Two dozen new members of Congress from the liberal Democratic side were elected in 1958, in part as a rebuke to the Eisenhower administration's short-lived intervention in Lebanon. The United States had recently concluded a stalemated war in Korea. But what was more important in the psyche of Americans was the Bomb. Whether in such films as *Dr. Strangelove,* or apocalyptic ones around coups by generals in the United States such as *Seven Days in May,* or end-of-the-world scenarios punctuated by the reality of school children hiding under their desks as protection against nuclear war, the nation was wrapped in insecurity. The Korean War was presented to the public as a "limited" war. But over 47,000 American soldiers died, as did over a million Koreans and hundreds of thousands of Chinese soldiers. The war ended in a truce in 1953, and to this day no peace treaty has been signed.

Nevertheless, there were shafts of light in Eisenhower's second term. In 1957 the Soviets and the Americans signed an agreement to abolish nuclear weapons in Western and Eastern Europe. This initial agreement was negotiated by Harold Stassen, Eisenhower's disarmament advisor. It was withdrawn by U.S. Secretary of State John Foster Dulles, however, who feared that any far-reaching agreement with the Soviets would weaken the NATO alliance and thereby jeopardize the American hold over Western Europe. This was epitomized by the bureaucratic slogan: "Keep Russia out, Americans in, and Germans down." Stassen, who took his role seriously, also hoped to derail Nixon's candidacy in 1960 for the presidency. But he had enemies, such as Henry Luce of *Time* and *Life,* who found Stassen a menace to Luce's view of the American century that in the minds of the imperialists of the time was based on military force, including nuclear weapons.

In 1959 the Soviets, following a plan first proposed in 1925 by Maxim Litvinov at the League of Nations, presented an outline for a program of complete and general disarmament. The Soviet government had also suspended nuclear testing in the atmosphere and cut hundreds of thousands of troops from its armed forces. It seemed to be a propitious time for what was later termed a "peace race," a phrase lifted from Seymour Melman, who became co-chair of SANE in the 1970s.

In Congress in 1959–60, political elites feared nuclear war more than they cared about the power of the Soviet Union. They believed that the United States needed an entirely different approach, whether it was peaceful competition or peaceful coexistence.

The Creation of the Arms Control and Disarmament Agency

As a general rule, Americans turn to reorganizations of government or adding to government with new agencies to "solve" a particular problem, whatever it might be. Thus, it was not surprising that there would be three proposals from the Democratic side that dealt with the organization of government for peace and disarmament.

The first proposal was presented by Sen. Hubert Humphrey of Minnesota, who chaired the Senate Foreign Relations Committee's subcommittee on disarmament. Humphrey held strongly to the idea of disengagement as a way of getting the Soviets out of Eastern Europe while disengaging American forces from Western Europe. He also believed strongly that a comprehensive program of economic conversion was necessary to avoid a depression or a recession. Arms buildups, thought Humphrey (and others associated with SANE), were sapping the strength of the United States in moral and economic terms. He wanted a strong institutional voice within any future administration to speak for a point of view that was different from the one held by the Department of Defense, the Joint Chiefs of Staff, and the Department of State.

The second proposal was put forward by Sen. John Kennedy of Massachusetts. It was far more modest and had the mark of the arms control seminar at Harvard, which meant that it was technocratically based. Members of the seminar—including Tom Schelling, McGeorge Bundy, Carl Kaysen, and Henry Kissinger—believed that armament and disarmament were highly technical questions that required great expertise. The Kennedy proposal revolved around the establishment of an arms control institute that would promote studies of "arms control" and policy directions that monitored and controlled the arms race so that war by mistake, miscalculation, or accident would not occur. The Kennedy proposal did not support disarmament, but rather attempted to rationalize the arms race into "manageable" proportions.

The third proposal adopted the systemic view advanced by Congressman Kastenmeier. He had proposed a peace agency that was far broader and would be concerned with the long and short term. It would have the president's ear directly, and, therefore, the agency would have a good chance of countering the arguments of the Department of Defense and the Department of State, for at certain meetings the director of the peace agency would be invited to the NSC for discussion and decision making. Furthermore, the agency would be a conduit for ideas and concerns of the public. I was one of the drafters of the appropriate legislation, and our intention was to promote an agency that adopted and created ideas that would set the "ship of state" on a far different course.

In 1961, the Arms Control and Disarmament Agency was established as a hybrid of these three legislative proposals. Critics of the idea said that there would be no way that such an agency of government would be able to counterbalance the Department of Defense. On the other hand, skeptics said it would be a place that would insulate the criticisms from the peace movement by steering criticism to the ACDA. In the beginning of the agency, the critics were only partially right. During its first few years, its staff included Freeman Dyson of the Institute for Advanced Study, Richard Barnet, Betty Goetz (Lall) of Sen. Humphrey's staff, and Louis Sohn of Harvard University. As the advisor on the NSC concerned with disarmament, I was the point of contact with the ACDA.

SANE and the Kennedy Administration

Thus, in the early 1960s, SANE was well positioned both in the White House and in the newly minted ACDA, which had direct access to the president under law, prepared papers for negotiation, and was central in the choice of the arms negotiator. It was hardly a surprise that Sandy Gottlieb and Norman Cousins would have an open door at the ACDA, for the time seemed ripe for fundamental changes. And it was gratifying to SANE members that Cousins was able to help craft some of the most important speeches given on disarmament and relations with the Soviet Union, notably the 1963 American University address that attempted to call off the Cold War. Of course, in history there are no guarantees. Success was not ensured just because there were people who spoke against war and indeed went to prison as conscientious objectors, or were tax resisters who undertook civil disobedience, or held academic seminars proving the harmful effects of fallout and the stupidity of aggressive wars, as others sought to work out the details of general disarmament treaties. Their actions, namely the actions of the concerned, faced the doctrines of McNamara, the "whiz kids," the uniformed military, and a nation intoxicated with military power, but enormously anxious as a result of military strategies for "world responsibility" ("imperialism" to the skeptical) guaranteed by an "open checkbook" that would prepare for every kind of war from sublimited to strategic nuclear war.

In Kennedy's "thousand days" before his assassination, the president came to believe that the way to change the Soviet Union was, not only through the project of spending the Soviets into bankruptcy, but through an end to a mutually destructive arms race. This was no easy matter, for he and his administration committed themselves to enormous increases in the defense budget. After the Cuban Missile Crisis, however, Kennedy, under pressure from inside the White House—notably Jerome Wiesner, the president's science advisor—maintained that an atmospheric nuclear test ban was possible and verifiable.

But that was only part of the story. It was SANE, Women Strike for Peace, and Linus Pauling who organized scientists against nuclear testing and nuclear war, and the public at large, especially women, who saw nuclear testing as destroying the lives of future generations of children and endangering their own children's lives. The revulsion against the Bomb in the popular mind took on a political presence that it did not seem to have under Eisenhower. It appeared to touch every family directly, whether through a farcical civil defense program or feelings of personal terror that gripped all sectors of American life and, indeed, the world around the Cuban Missile Crisis and around the mutual threats between the Soviet and U.S. governments over Berlin.

During this period, peace groups and especially SANE saw the possibilities of two strategies, which their members and leadership hoped would be complementary. One was the immediate incremental step—to end nuclear testing. But that was merely to be a door opener. The next steps would lead to serious negotiations for general and complete disarmament. The reader will no doubt wonder at the naïveté of this writer and of the time. But it is important to remember that the United States and the Soviet Union had negotiated eight principles that were to serve as a framework for comprehensive disarmament negotiations. The United States and the Soviets jointly presented this framework agreement to the United Nations and serious negotiations began in 1962 under the 18 nation Geneva disarmament talks, co-chaired by the United States and the Soviet Union. SANE, too, adopted a general and complete disarmament position, although it emphasized more immediate and seemingly attainable goals.

Through a series of well-constructed ads and lobbying among different groups, the work of Gottlieb and Cousins proved successful in ending nuclear testing in the atmosphere. But the project did not reach its full potential for reasons outside the control of the peace movement and SANE. Thanks to Soviet-American disagreements over inspection, the nuclear test ban treaty of 1963 was a truncated arrangement, for it applied only to testing in the atmosphere, under the sea, and in outer space. And this meant that, as an arms control and disarmament program, the treaty was not successful, for it did not end nuclear testing underground. Whether a stronger and more vociferous peace movement could have forced a comprehensive nuclear test ban is not clear, although there were pockets in the government (the ACDA and the White House) that would have welcomed large-scale demonstrations to press the issue.

The peace movement, which had hoped that the atmospheric test ban would be an incremental step to general disarmament, was disabused of that possibility by those in Congress and the administration who were eager to limit its purpose and escape the road to general disarmament. President Kennedy was caught in the vise of a huge defense buildup under Defense Secretary McNamara and the Joint Chiefs. They spurned the disarmament program that the Soviets had asked for as a next step: namely a nonaggression pact between NATO and Warsaw Pact nations. The Soviet proposal also had little support among NATO allies.

The Impact of the Vietnam War

Whatever progress there might have been toward general disarmament was interrupted with the death of Kennedy. Vice President Lyndon Johnson, like most American political leaders, including some who had supported disarmament, believed in the "domino theory." In the case of Indochina, this meant that, if that country was lost to the Communist or indigenous popular forces, the entire hegemonic position of the United States would be lost to the Soviet Union and Communist China. In the early 1960s, American leaders and the press saw China and the Soviet Union as inseparable twins joined at the ideological and geopolitical hip. Such was the level of sophistication of American policymakers after the purges of State Department experts.

As a result of the Indochina war, the angle of SANE's concern changed. SANE was faced with the double question of how to confront

SANE holds a March on Washington for Peace in Vietnam, in Washington, D.C., on November 27, 1965. Drawing an estimated 35,000 participants, it was the largest public protest thus far against the war *(records of SANE, Swarthmore College Peace Collection)*.

the escalating war and how to present itself as a concerned, some said "responsible middle class," peace movement that would appeal to a broad-based constituency that wanted access to Congress and the Johnson administration. Much concern was given to the question of how not to appear as crazies and fringe people, although SANE was 180 degrees opposite to that charge in style and demeanor.

Nevertheless, the task of positioning was a complex one, for it meant holding on to different elements of the broader peace movement. This included young activists broadly identified with the "New Left," radical nonviolent activists best reflected in the positions taken by Muste, members of Congress (for example, Sens. Ernest Gruening and Wayne Morse), and internationally known figures (including Cousins and Spock, each of whom held different points of view in terms of organizing and appeal). The breakdown in communication and the internal schism that resulted from differences over an appropriate approach to the war adversely affected SANE's position as the center of resistance against war and nuclearism.

It was during this period, after the signing of the nuclear test ban agreement in 1963, that SANE began to decline. The blame for this decline cannot be placed at the doorstep of the SANE leadership or its board. In fact, under the leadership of Gottlieb, attempts were made, some prescient and successful, to find the proper balance between demonstrations and patriotic responsibility during a war thrust upon American society by the U.S. government.

Most of SANE's membership supported Lyndon Johnson in the 1964 presidential campaign. But by 1965 SANE's honeymoon with Johnson and Humphrey had ended, as Johnson pressed ahead with an expanded war in Indochina and sponsored military intervention in the Dominican Republic. The respect that Dr. Spock and other members of the SANE board and staff felt for Johnson ended as the Johnson administration lost moral and political legitimacy. This was another tragic moment in American politics, for the war and the Johnson administration's willful misunderstanding of what was happening in Indochina aborted the political work tying civil rights to disarmament and economic and social justice with support from what Johnson supporters had believed would be a liberal-minded administration that would be open and welcoming to liberalism as a populist and radical force. They hoped it would have a more powerful, positive effect on American society than Roosevelt's New Deal. But, instead, American liberalism was shaken to its roots. SANE undertook direct opposition to the Johnson government's war position on the grounds that it was folly and the betrayal of what was best in modern liberalism. Personally, I concluded that the American state had become a national security state that had to be transformed and dismantled.

SANE's emphasis changed as it moved to a position of direct confrontation with the government. Stopping the war in Indochina required a new strategy. The pendulum had swung, and while the Soviet Union was understood by many in SANE as a profoundly negative force, others now saw it as merely a junior partner attempting to keep up with the arms race of which the American national security state served as the engine.

More than others, Gottlieb steered the direction of SANE organizationally during most of the 1960s. His purpose was one of rational prudence in a time when the most profound changes seemed to defy that feature of leadership. The New Left claimed that the priorities of any organization that perceived the Soviet Union as a direct threat to the United States missed the actual power constellations in the world. It was the American administration with its penchant for war that had become a threat to the United States and the world. Furthermore, many in SANE took their cues from Martin Luther King Jr. and Muste, who called for nonviolent resistance as an effective tool and a badge of honor. Indeed, the rhythm of American left-of-center politics was captured by

H. Stuart Hughes, SANE co-chair, presents Harry Belafonte and Coretta Scott King with a posthumous award to Martin Luther King Jr., December 1969 *(records of SANE, Swarthmore College Peace Collection)*.

King, himwself a SANE supporter. There was a concerted effort on the part of some associated with SANE to run King and Spock for president and vice president in 1968.

Perhaps most important was the position on the war taken by SANE, at the urging of Gottlieb. SANE had hoped for a negotiated settlement with the National Liberation Front (NLF) and the North Vietnamese. But that position (held until 1965 by this writer and by Bernard Fall, who together edited the *Vietnam Reader*) was flawed and unworkable as the war continued. The fact was that, under the Geneva Accords, an election was supposed to have been held in Vietnam in 1956. But the United States refused to honor the Geneva agreement. Anything less than keeping that commitment would prove to be a failure, as it was.

By 1967, members of SANE and of the broader peace move-ment—including William Sloane Coffin Jr., Melman, Spock, and this author—called for the indictment of American government officials who waged an illegal, immoral, and unconstitutional war. Melman had compiled several hundred pages of raw reports from newspaper accounts of alleged American war crimes. Indeed, the *Pentagon Papers* reaffirmed much of what the broadened peace movement said. Along with Spock, Coffin, Mitchell Goodman, and Michael Ferber, I stood trial and was acquitted for conspiracy and counseling young men to evade the draft. The trial grew out of draft card turn-ins and a document that Arthur Waskow (who later became a rabbi) and I wrote, entitled the "Call to Resist Illegitimate Authority." Many members of SANE signed the statement as it became clear that what was at stake was the meaning of democracy itself, under threat from the military-industrial complex Eisenhower had warned against and the expanded national security state that burdened American and international life beyond what Eisenhower would have imagined.

In retrospect, SANE was our movement home, and most of us never left it.

Chapter 5

SANE Reborn

David Cortright

"Is SANE still around?" This is what I asked myself in 1977, when members of the SANE board of directors asked me to become executive director. SANE had played an important historic role in halting atmospheric nuclear testing and was an early opponent of the Vietnam War, but the organization had not been active in recent years. The board members painted a glowing picture of a venerable organization with a great potential for future achievement, so I decided to accept the position. When I arrived at the SANE offices, however, I was shocked to see the paltry state of the organization and the meager condition of its finances. "This could be the shortest job on record," I thought to myself. Only two staff remained, and the active membership list, which in SANE's heyday stood at more than 25,000, had dwindled to just a few thousand. Not only was the organization out of money, it owed the Internal Revenue Service $10,000 in unpaid back taxes. As the end of the year approached with the government threatening to shut us down, it seemed that the end was indeed near. Suddenly an anonymous $10,000 contribution arrived, which we promptly used to pay the taxes. Fortune smiled on us again when we applied to the post office for a third-class bulk mail permit, which would reduce the cost of mailings but was difficult to obtain. When I mentioned to the skeptical postal official that Norman Thomas was one of SANE's founders, his eyes lit up and his previously stern countenance softened. Explaining how his family had been long-time supporters of the Socialist Party, he gushed forth his admiration for "the great Norman Thomas" and promptly approved the mail permit. We were in business, debt free, and ready to begin investing in a direct mail campaign to recruit new members.

A Convincing, Coherent Political Program and a Co-chair to Match

Before SANE could attract renewed support, we needed an innovative political program that could generate enthusiasm and excitement among potential members. Organizational development efforts depend upon the existence of a convincing, coherent political program. For SANE in the late 1970s, that meant a focus on economic conversion. The political moment was right in the early years of the Carter administration. The SALT I agreement and the political backlash against the Vietnam War had led to some moderation in military spending levels and raised anew the challenge of providing alternatives for workers and communities that are dependent on the war economy. SANE had the right leadership for such an effort in the person of the national co-chair, economist Seymour Melman, one of the world's foremost experts on conversion issues. With Melman's knowledge and authority on the issue and SANE's history of working in Washington for constructive alternatives to militarism, the organization was well positioned to build a campaign for conversion.

The decisive factor in generating enthusiasm for the economic conversion program was the leadership of William Winpisinger, the newly elected president of the International Association of Machinists. Winpisinger had ascended through the ranks of the Machinists Union and was relatively unknown when he became president in 1977. Politically progressive and committed to peace and justice, Winpisinger courageously supported nuclear disarmament and the conversion of military industries, despite the fact that many of his own union members worked in missile and aerospace plants.

Seymour Melman, SANE's new co-chair, in February 1974 *(records of SANE, Swarth-more College Peace Collection)*.

I had heard Winpisinger speak during a symposium soon after he took office, and I was both amazed and impressed to hear this head of a major military-sector union advocate a program of arms reduction and economic conversion. My interest in taking the position at SANE was motivated in part by a passion for economic conversion and the hope that Winpisinger might become a partner in a conversion campaign. Soon after I started at SANE, Melman and I went to see Winpisinger and asked him to serve as co-chair of the organization. We proposed that he join us in leading a new labor-peace alliance for economic conversion. We told him of our dream of SANE and the Machinists working together to build a campaign for reversing the arms race and redirecting economic resources from the arms sector to more productive civilian purposes. Winpisinger readily agreed and through his aides Richard Greenwood and Barbara Shailor co-chaired the organization for the next decade, helping to create new political energy for the peace movement. With the labor-peace alliance for conversion as our program and Winpisinger as a dynamic new leader, SANE began to attract renewed interest and support. By 1979 membership levels were starting to rise, foundation grants and major contributions were pouring in, and an energetic new staff was emerging.

The economic conversion program propelled SANE forward for a couple of years, but it could not be sustained in the face of deteriorating political conditions in Washington and the reemergence of a Cold War atmosphere. In the aftermath of the Soviet invasion of Afghanistan and the Iranian revolution, and with the prodding of a well-organized right-wing campaign, U.S. policymakers reversed the direction of military policy and began to increase military spending and the development of nuclear weapons. Planning for the conversion of military bases and production plants no longer made sense and dropped off the political agenda. Public policy moved in the opposite direction, toward greater rather than less investment in militarism. Nuclear weapons dangers sharply increased as the Carter administration proposed building the MX mobile missile system and decided to deploy Intermediate-range Nuclear Forces (INF) in Europe.

Antinuclear sentiment deepened, however, in the wake of the 1979 nuclear accident at Three Mile Island. The Reagan administration fueled public fear when it sharply increased military spending. Reckless and ill-informed statements by the president and his advisers struck terror in the hearts of millions. A Pentagon directive called for "prevailing" in a nuclear war, and the secretary of state spoke of nuclear warning shots.

William Winpisinger, president of the International Association of Machinists and SANE's co-chair *(records of SANE, Swarthmore College Peace Collection)*.

A New Political Program

In this climate of rising public anxiety, the driving motivation for peace activism shifted from hope to fear. We turned from working for peaceful alternatives to campaigning against renewed nuclear dangers. In this setting, the "Call to Halt the Nuclear Arms Race," issued by Randy Forsberg, struck a responsive chord and attracted immediate public support. The Nuclear Weapons Freeze Campaign emerged in response to Forsberg's call to become the embodiment of the growing public opposition to nuclear weapons. SANE and other existing peace groups supported the Freeze and in some cases helped to build the campaign, in my case by serving on the initial Nuclear Freeze Strategy Committee. SANE and other groups benefited enormously from the rise of the Freeze Campaign. We were able to ride a wave of widespread public support for disarmament and took advantage of unprecedented opportunities for organizational growth and increased political influence. SANE also began to focus on stopping the first-strike MX missile system as a specific and achievable step toward halting the arms race.

Membership Recruitment and Canvassing

As the Nuclear Freeze campaign took off, SANE launched a large-scale program of membership recruitment and organizational development. We recognized, in the tradition of Saul Alinsky, that organizational clout is necessary to bring about social change and achieve political influence. The freeze movement was plowing fertile ground for planting the seeds of organizational growth. Public opinion polls showed a majority of Americans supporting a halt to the arms race. Nuclear freeze groups were popping up all over the country and in some cases were forming regional and state campaigns, but no effort was being made to harness this political energy into sustained membership growth and organizational clout. At SANE we decided to focus our energies on building a broad national membership base for disarmament. We invested heavily in direct mail programs that brought in thousands of additional donors and members.

In 1983 we accelerated our membership recruitment efforts by creating a door-to-door canvassing program. The SANE program was established on the basis of the successful model developed by the Citizen Action network, which had created large-scale citizen groups in more than a dozen states through the use of paid canvassers. The SANE program grew rapidly and by 1985 had offices in a dozen cities and a staff during summer peak months of more than 200 canvassers. Each night SANE canvassers were reaching thousands of households and recruiting hundreds of new members. Membership levels rose sharply, jumping from approximately 5,000 in the late 1970s to nearly 150,000 by the mid-1980s. We also created a telemarketing program, again following the Citizen Action model, signing up thousands of newly recruited members to become monthly sustainers. Membership income increased dramatically and the SANE budget reached nearly $5 million in 1986. Managing the huge costs of the canvass and the rapid expansion in membership proved beyond our capabilities, however, and exacerbated financial problems a few years later when the ending of the Cold War and the consequent lowering of public concern reduced contribution levels.

Rapid Response Network versus First-Strike MX

As membership and income increased in the early 1980s, so did our organizational presence and political clout on Capitol Hill. The SANE staff expanded rapidly to include additional lobbyists, organizers, and a communications team. The organizing staff established a Rapid Response Network of tens of thousands of members in targeted congressional districts who could be mobilized quickly to exert pressure on Congress during key legislative votes. The SANE offices often buzzed with energy in the evening as volunteers made phone calls to activate telephone trees in hundreds of communities around the country, which could produce hundreds and even thousands of overnight calls to targeted legislators on specific issues. We established a political action committee to participate in elections and raise money from our members on behalf of progressive candidates. These efforts helped to translate public support for ending the arms race into organized political pressure in Washington. Lobbyists for SANE, the Nuclear Weapons Freeze Campaign, the Council for a Livable World, and other groups, became important players in shaping arms control legislation. We activated the growing grassroots disarmament constituency to build opposition to the MX missile system, nuclear weapons testing, and the Reagan administration's Strategic Defense Initiative (Star Wars). Our strategy of building political influence through organizational clout was beginning to pay dividends, as opposition to the Reagan nuclear buildup and support for arms control increased at the grassroots level and on Capitol Hill.

The campaign against the MX missile was a key element in the revival of SANE. This gargantuan nuclear missile system, proposed by the Carter administration, was projected to be the largest weapons program in history. The mobile basing plan was conceived as a giant shell game in which 200 missiles with ten hydrogen bombs each would shuttle among 4,600 missile shelters along 10,000 miles of heavy-duty roadway in 200 race tracks built in the Great Basin area of Nevada and Utah. The proposed system was so large and unwieldy and had so many likely negative consequences that it might collapse of its own weight, especially if given a push by effective citizen opposition. It was a preposterous and dangerous program, truly insane, that provided an inviting political target. SANE and other groups made stopping the MX a top priority. Focusing on the MX allowed SANE to create a niche for itself within the larger arms control community and the emerging Nuclear Freeze Campaign. It also offered an opportunity to establish political credentials on Capitol Hill, among grassroots activists, and within the affected communities in the Great Basin region. The campaign against the MX missile provided an extraordinary coalition-building opportunity, leading to a remarkable political partnership among unlikely allies. Native American groups opposed to the desecration of tribal lands, trade unions, and taxpayer groups concerned about the waste of money, Nevada and Utah ranchers defending grazing rights, Mormon church leaders worried about threats to their traditional way of life—all these joined with SANE, the Council for a Livable World, Friends of the Earth, and arms control legislators on Capitol Hill to defeat the mobile missile system. Ronald Reagan canceled the mobile basing system in October 1981. The success of the MX campaign was a great victory for all who participated. It also helped to build SANE's reputation and established political relationships that proved valuable in subsequent years.

Cancellation of the mobile basing plan did not put an end to the MX missile program. Although no basing plan existed for the missile, the Reagan administration and the Air Force continued to push for its production and deployment. The campaign against the MX now moved to Capitol Hill, where we fought to defeat the missile through a cutoff of production funds. Some of the partners in the first phase of the campaign dropped out, but most of the participating groups, and others that later joined, continued the fight, which became one of the largest, most sustained arms control lobbying campaigns in history. The battle over the MX missile dominated the arms control debate in Washington for five years, with SANE and other arms control groups at the center of the struggle. It was in this phase of the campaign that Common Cause brought its considerable lobbying acumen and muscle to the fray. The White House, the Air Force, and the military–industrial complex put their full weight behind the missile program, but the anti-MX coalition succeeded in whittling away missile funding and eventually reduced it to one quarter its original scale. The campaign not only brought partial success and prevented the deployment of a destabilizing first-strike missile system, but proved beneficial for raising funds, recruiting and activating members, building coalitions, and strengthening organizational networks. It played a key role in forging an effective arms control lobby on Capitol Hill.

A Campaign Against Nuclear Testing

Even more important than the MX battle in building SANE and the broader peace movement was the campaign against nuclear testing. The struggle to halt the testing of nuclear weapons had been a central concern of the disarmament movement since the beginning of the atomic age. It was one of the primary concerns that prompted the founding of SANE in 1957. It reemerged as a dominant issue in the 1980s as a way of giving concrete expression to the public demand for a nuclear freeze. The Nuclear Weapons Freeze Campaign needed a specific, realistic political objective to sustain the momentum of the movement after the disappointing congressional debate in 1983, when a watered-down freeze resolution was passed in the House of Representatives but was rejected in the Senate. Many of us argued that a focused campaign to halt nuclear testing would offer an achievable political objective as the first step toward implementing a nuclear freeze. In the spring of 1985, SANE and the Nuclear Weapons Freeze Campaign joined to launch a nationwide petition campaign to halt nuclear testing. We set a goal of collecting one million signatures by the time of the scheduled Reagan-Gorbachev summit in November 1985. The importance of the test ban issue and enthusiasm for the SANE-Freeze petition increased dramatically when Soviet leader Mikhail Gorbachev announced a unilateral Soviet moratorium on nuclear testing in August 1985, on the 40th anniversary of the atomic bombing of Hiroshima. Our political message was simple and effective: the United States should reply positively to the Soviet initiative, saying "yes" to the Soviet "da." The public response to the petition was strong, and SANE canvassers and local freeze organizers were able to reach the goal of one million signatures in just a few months.

The call to halt nuclear testing as the first step toward a nuclear freeze was the primary political theme of the SANE canvass. Tens of thousands of new members were recruited on the basis of the 1985 petition drive and continuing efforts to halt U.S. nuclear testing. No other issue was more popular with people at the doors or more effective in building membership. The test ban campaign also solidified the partnership between SANE and the Freeze Campaign that became the basis for organizational merger. The entire nuclear freeze movement supported the test ban campaign. Thousands of activists (including Freeze director Jane Gruenebaum and myself) trekked to the Nevada nuclear weapons test site to participate in massive civil disobedience actions against nuclear testing. A major lobbying campaign developed to force a U.S. response to the Soviet moratorium by getting Congress to cut off appropriations for further nuclear testing. Tens of thousands of local activists contacted their legislators to urge support. An amendment to deny funds for nuclear testing was approved by the House of Representatives in August 1986 by a 234–155 margin. Similar measures were approved by the House in 1987 and 1988, although in each case the Senate did not concur and the legislation died. In 1992 both the House and the Senate approved legislation halting nuclear tests, which the first President Bush reluctantly signed into law in October—a major victory for the peace movement and a giant step toward halting the nuclear arms race.

A Focused Political Program and a Membership Program

The revival of SANE was based on two interrelated principles—the importance of building membership, and the need for a focused political program. The two are intimately linked and must be pursued together to establish political influence. In the early years, 1978–80, the labor-peace alliance for economic conversion provided the political focus, while direct mailings served as the principal means of recruiting new members and donors. During most of the 1980s, the political program shifted toward support for a nuclear weapons freeze in general and a halt to nuclear testing in particular. The door-to-door canvass became the principal means of recruiting new members and generating grassroots pressure. The anti–MX missile campaign was successful in constraining the nuclear weapons buildup. It also helped in establishing SANE's political credentials, building coalitions, and strengthening grassroots action networks. By tapping into rising public anxiety about nuclear dangers and by offering a realistic program for step-by-step progress toward peace, SANE was able to build institutional clout and contribute to the historic citizens' movement that helped to end the Cold War.

Chapter 6

How the Freeze Campaign's Unifying Idea Empowered Us

Patricia McCullough

The Berrigan brothers, those radical antiwar priests in the 1960s, changed my life. A chance purchase of Daniel Berrigan's *They Call Us Dead Men* in a graduate school bookstore startled me into seeing the Gospels and being faithful in a totally different framework. It was a "paradigm shift"—surprising, even unwanted—that left me more clear-sighted but alone. In that personal aloneness, I read almost frantically on peace and justice. My husband, a West Point graduate, came back from Vietnam and gave three dynamic speeches against the war; that gave me more encouragement. I attended the Catholic "Call to Action" meeting in Detroit and was deeply moved to further action after hearing a priest challenge the audience with the question: "What will you tell your children when they ask you, 'Mom and Dad, why didn't you do anything about the arms race?'" As a mother of four, I knew it was time to act.

But it wasn't until I arrived in Louisville, Kentucky, three years later, that I was finally fortunate enough to join with others similarly seeking a way to "incarnate" their understanding of faith in light of the accelerating nuclear arms race. We began a Mobilization for Survival group in Louisville. It met each month in my living room, a small but hopeful beginning. However, we were like the proverbial "Six Characters in Search of an Author." We lacked a narrative framework that engaged our audiences. We struggled for the message that would indeed "mobilize" people to resist an arms race that was literally threatening "survival." We tried to organize for the SALT treaties but that was like talking Greek to audiences, and not Biblical Greek at that. The SALT II Treaty was complex and people's eyes would glaze over when we explained it.

Then, in 1979, our Mobilization for Survival group hosted the annual national meeting of the "Mobe," in Louisville. It was at this conference that Randy Forsberg announced her proposal for the Freeze—a bilateral halt in the testing, development, and deployment of nuclear weapons: no more focusing just on stopping the MX missile, only to have three other new weapons pop up even if we won against the MX. The Freeze said both sides had far more than enough nuclear weapons to destroy each other many times over. It was pointless to argue about details of who was ahead with one weapon or another. Both sides should simply halt their development of nuclear weapons where they were: Stop. Freeze.

The response was electric. People were talking about how much sense Randy's proposal made. I was enthusiastic, and I told Randy so—she was staying in my home. I was particularly struck with the strength of the proposal that a Freeze would stop the development of highly destabilizing "first-strike weapons." First-strike weapons like the MX were so accurate that they could hit and eliminate the other side's deterrent weapons capacity. That would undermine what stability there was in deterrence. The crazy but useful justification for not using nuclear weapons was that there was no advantage to using nuclear weapons first because the other side would retaliate with massive destruction, even after being struck, because their arsenal would still be intact even if their country was not. But now accurate and multiple-warhead first-strike nuclear weapons could actually destroy the ability to retaliate. The dynamic would shift to acting first so as not to lose one's weapons, rather than not acting at all for fear of retaliation. Once this was clearly described and understood, the rationale for an escalating arms race was seen to be what it was: Insane.

I remember meeting with Sen. Wendell Ford of Kentucky. We learned that he was opposing the Freeze because he thought nuclear weapons were like new models of cars: Newer ones are better than older ones. So we explained that the newer ones would move us to first-strike capability and be enormously destabilizing. We saw the light turn on for him. After that, he supported the Freeze.

My contribution, with Glen Stassen, was to persuade Randy Forsberg and Chris Payne, a nuclear weapons expert, to write the Euromissiles into the Freeze proposal. The Euromissiles (Pershing II and ground-launched nuclear-tipped cruise missiles, and Soviet SS-4s, SS-5s, and SS-20s) were the most destabilizing of all the missile developments. The Pershing II and cruise missiles would be enormously threatening to the Soviet nuclear command and control center near Moscow; but they would be stored in highly visible above-ground storage depots, in West Germany, Italy, Holland, Belgium, and Britain, where the Soviet Union could quickly destroy them in a crisis. It was an invitation for beginning a nuclear shootout at the OK Corral. Including the Euromissiles in the Freeze, not only made conceptual sense, but linked the U.S. Freeze campaign to the European antinuclear groups.

I had the privilege of speaking to the German groups protesting the Pershing II missiles. It was thrilling to hear 4,000 German protesters cheer at a rally when I explained the Freeze and how blocking the Euromissiles was an integral part of our campaign. I certainly wasn't John F. Kennedy, but this is a moment I will remember for a lifetime. On another European trip to England, I teamed up with an American Methodist minister and activist to speak to church groups about the Freeze and the European weapons. The most deeply inspiring event was sharing time and discussion with the women at the Greenham Common protest camp. Greenham Common was the site of a U.S. Air Force base where cruise missiles were to be deployed. Construction of the site was well under way, and the women—ranging from young students to grandmothers—were trying to stop it, despite the "imbalance of power." In the bitterly cold British winter, they set up a makeshift camp of plastic tents each night, only to have them torn down each morning by the British police. Nevertheless, month after month of the protest, the proper British delivered the mail and picked up the garbage! During my stay, we sat on hay barrels drinking tea around a campfire. I have never been simultaneously so cold and so warmed in heart by their fierce dedication to having cruise missiles removed from the base and, thus, their beautiful countryside removed as a Soviet target. I drew on their inspiring and courageous example many times in the years to come when my own spirits lagged, confronted by the enormity of the opposition. A group of ragged and committed women confronted the mighty British government and made it blink. Now all Euromissiles—all medium-range nuclear missiles—are gone. It was perhaps the biggest victory of the Freeze.

Organizing for Lasting Power

Before the Freeze Campaign got under way, three Episcopal priests in Louisville attended an Episcopalian Urban Ministry Conference and were fired up by an address in which the Rev. George Regas of All Saints Church in Pasadena presented the challenge of reversing the arms race. They asked for help from our small Mobe group. Together we organized a new ecumenical organization, the Louisville Area Council on Peacemaking and Religion. The ministers brought the clout of church leadership and organized a board with a respected member from each major church denomination, selected by that denomination. We brought knowledge of the nuclear arms race, and maybe more important, knowledge of how to organize an ongoing and lasting movement. So we became the steering committee, under the authority of the board. After the Freeze Campaign began, the council grew to 3,000 members. They couldn't fit in my living room anymore. The Freeze caught on with the people so well because of its clarity, simplicity, and unity; it enabled us to multiply our membership a hundredfold.

I can remember speaking to many church groups on arms control before the Freeze was announced. Educated Episcopal and Presbyterian congregations were particularly interested, but the discussions quickly became very intellectual and abstract. We felt a certain helplessness in the face of the complexity without clear alternatives. The only thing I had going for me was a relentless sense of "we gotta do something." After the Freeze was announced it became so much easier and more persuasive. Most important, the sense of helplessness was lifted. We could do something clear, sensible, and "for sure," as the kids say. As a sense of empowerment grew, we were able to expand beyond regularly scheduled church meeting times to intentionally scheduled house meetings on the Freeze.

My own role was executive director of the Louisville Area Council of Peacemaking and Religion. Others may connect with other constituencies, but our strategy was to be clear about our base, suggested by those Episcopal priests. We were interreligious, Christian and Jewish, and fortunate to have representatives on our board from all major denominations. This provided us with access to discuss the faith implications of the nuclear arms race, organizational strength in our ongoing connection with churches and synagogues, and long-lasting staying power. Many dedicated people spoke out because of their faith to other church members in an informed way with a viable proposal—the Freeze. We provided accurate and reliable materials to make presentations interesting and understandable.

Nationally, professional groups were organizing around the Freeze and against the spiraling arms race. The associate director of the council, Terry Weiss, ably gathered Physicians for Social Responsibility, Lawyers for Social Responsibility, and Educators for Social Responsibility into articulate, organized groups. Ongoing small groups were organized in churches under the guidance of Glen Stassen, whose book, *Journey Into Peacemaking*—based on the small-group strategy of what is now Every Church a Peace Church (www.ecapc.org)—became the manual for the groups.

The Catholic bishops' pastoral letter, "The Challenge of Peace," which endorsed the Freeze, greatly assisted our work, primarily because our archbishop, Thomas Kelly, took it seriously. He organized meetings of the diocesan clergy to discuss the pastoral and its implications for the arms race. He and I appeared on radio and TV shows locally to bring peacemaking "into the pews" as a personal matter of faith for parish members. Many parishes hosted meetings, and the people were beginning to talk about moral issues related to the arms race. "Leave it to the experts" was changing to "this is a serious matter of faith and we can't remain silent." Everybody could be an "expert" once they understood that the Freeze enhanced security, whereas letting the arms race run wild could bring untold destruction. Monsignor Alfred Horrigan, founder and past president of Bellarmine College, worked tirelessly to provide access to groups and individual donors. Sister Mary Schmuck, RSM, an energetic, knowledgeable, and faithful worker, became a key member of the steering committee. She wrote a monthly newsletter filled with peacemaking information for her nationwide religious order.

The Council on Peacemaking and Religion held its regular monthly meetings at our host church, Christ Church Cathedral, where our founding members, the Very Rev. Allen Bartlett Jr. and the Rev. Spenser Simrill, were dean and canon. A speaker would address a topic of importance to our work, and then six action groups with their own action foci would meet and plan. At these meetings and major community forums, such speakers as William Sloane Coffin Jr., Carl Sagan, Helen Caldicott, and my own heroes, Philip and Daniel Berrigan, spoke. Jim Wallis, author of the recent best seller, *God's Politics*, came to Louisville more than once, spoke in churches and in the seminaries, and made a big impact. One of the action groups, dedicated to education on peacemaking and alternative ways to handle conflict, became a Quaker-funded project supporting the implementation of conflict resolution and peer mediation, and its curriculum is still going strong in the Jefferson County school system. Another group teaches conflict and mediation skills to Louisvillians and contracts with the Louisville Housing Authority to resolve tenants' debt problems in public housing. The main thrust of the council continues as Interfaith Paths to Peace—continuing the faith-based organizing but now with additional faith-diversity—especially important after the U.S. government turned the response to the 9-11 attack into a permanent "war on terror." Our organizing has had staying power because it was deeply embedded in ongoing churches, faith organizations, and schools.

Why Did the Freeze Catch On So Well?
Why Did It Help Local Grassroots
Groups Like Ours Multiply?

1. It was a clear message that *unified the whole antinuclear movement*. All campaigns, such as against the MX missile, the B-2 bomber, and the medium-range Euromissiles, were incorporated into this one, clear, unifying message. No longer were we a scattered conglomeration of different campaigns about different weapons. All were unified by our one, clear, long-range strategy.

When I served as co-chair of the executive committee of the national Freeze Campaign, I can remember our working together to maintain the unity of focus and to articulate the message in direct and easily understood ways. Flip charts were designed to emphasize the importance of the Freeze and the ability to verify compliance. The flip charts showed how many nuclear weapons (about 400) would destroy the Soviet Union and showed the huge number of superfluous, dangerous, and highly costly nuclear weapons the U.S. and Soviet governments had. It was easy for us to articulate in church basements. People got the message. They understood it. They signed up. Our membership multiplied.

2. It was a radical message that *would make a major difference for values that people cared about.* It would entirely stop the nuclear weapons race. It would save billions of dollars. It would prevent the development of more dangerous and destabilizing weapons. So it would make a major difference for our security, and for the waste of billions of dollars on eternally developing more and more nuclear weapons. We met occasionally with the editors of the *Louisville Courier-Journal*, successfully encouraging them to write editorials. They knew we were connecting with their readers' values and knew that we were informed. We also got our own guest editorials published and got on television talk shows.

3. It *addressed values and concerns of conservatives* who feared that if we stopped this or that weapon, the Soviets might get ahead. The Freeze was bilateral; both sides would stop simultaneously. Once a group of Freeze advocates met with the Republican congressman from Lexington. He was opposing the Freeze. We said to him, "It is a *mutual, bilateral* Freeze." But we sensed that he still thought the peace movement favored unilateral disarmament. So one of us said it even more simply: "If the Soviets don't freeze, we won't freeze." He said, "What? If the Soviets don't freeze, we won't freeze?" We said, "Yes, if the Soviets don't freeze, we won't freeze." He said, "Oh! Then I can support it." All the Freeze literature had said "mutual," "bilateral" freeze, but he had not caught on. He was too stuck with his stereotypes; it took personal and direct clarification to break that misconception.

The Freeze focused only on what was verifiable: we would halt *testing, production, and deployment* of nuclear weapons—which could be easily verified. We would not halt secret research in the laboratory. It did not depend on "trusting the Russians." We had graphic flip charts showing the spy satellites, the worldwide seismographs, and the electronic and radio interception that enabled the CIA to know if the Soviet Union tested a new missile or a new nuclear weapon. We explained that producing nuclear weapons is not a cottage industry; it's big; it gives off evidence. The United States had the technical means to check whether cheating was occurring. Every new nuclear weapons system that the Soviet Union developed had been announced by the CIA even before it was tested. And deployment of just one missile in its silo took the excavation of 200 truckloads of dirt, the installation of huge amounts of cement and electronic equipment, and the trucking in of the huge missile. Our spy satellites observed all this. We knew exactly where every Soviet missile was and exactly how many there were. I used concrete examples learned from one of my professors at the University of Louisville: U.S. spy satellites could almost "see the time on a Russian general's watch, and read a license plate in Moscow."

In addition to some technical language, we also allowed the language of emotion and morals to enter the discussions. Someone said: "If destroying the world with nuclear weapons isn't worth getting emotional about, what is?" So those of us from the council got less technical and more relational and spoke of children, creation, and the suffering of people and programs hurt by budget cuts to human needs. The cost of the military budget at that time was about $300 billion a year. We got people's attention by breaking that down to cost per hour.

4. The national Freeze Campaign *supported local groups like ours and assisted in getting groups started in other states.* At one point, a Catholic expert on ethics and international relations, Bryan Hehir, remarked that there were more "Freeze groups than post offices" around the country. Randy Kehler, executive director of the national Freeze Campaign, was not only good at organizational work but sensitive relationally. When he stayed in my home in Louisville on a visit, I remember how very kind he was to my young daughter, Laura. Daniel Ellsberg's book *Secrets: A Memoir of Vietnam and the Pentagon Papers* has a picture of Randy with the caption: "Randy Kehler giving the talk at Haverford College on August 28, 1969, that opened my eyes to the possibilities of resisting war."

I hope that Peace Action can develop a clear, unifying strategy that brings together the various peace campaigns, that makes sense to people, that makes a major difference for the values they care about, and that is achievable. That way, ordinary folks like me will climb on board knowing that our efforts can make a major difference for what we really care about. We may not be experts, but we know that an overall, unifying strategy can make life a lot safer for our children and grandchildren.

Chapter 7

The Freeze Grassroots Strategy

Building the Movement

Ben Senturia in Consultation with Randy Kehler

During its short reign the Freeze was the largest American grassroots peace campaign of recent times, with millions of supporters, major media attention, and a significant amount of money. It spread across the country like wildfire because of the unique circumstances of the times and because of the Freeze's grassroots strategy. It succeeded in forcing Ronald Reagan to negotiate with Mikhail Gorbachev, which led to halting the nuclear arms spiral. It activated a generation of Americans.

But after 1983, the grassroots power of the movement dissipated. By the time the Freeze merged with SANE it had lost much of its grassroots strength. Could the Freeze have had an even greater impact on the country? What might have extended its length of influence?[1]

Freeze Background

In the late 1970s and early 1980s, conditions were ripe for the Freeze proposal and debate. New nuclear weapons were mushrooming in an out-of-control, escalating nuclear arms race: the MX, ABM, B-1 bomber, Trident II, cruise missile, and Pershing II missile. The Committee on the Present Danger was fanning the flames of fear about Soviet nuclear weapons. The peace community's campaigns to halt the onrush of new weapons met with some success, but without an appealing focus or galvanizing issue, the community was limited.

In 1979 Randy Forsberg proposed the concept of a freeze at a meeting of Mobilization for Survival. It called on the United States and the Soviet Union to adopt a mutual freeze on all further testing, production, and deployment of nuclear weapons and their delivery systems.

In March 1981, more than 300 people gathered at Georgetown University for the first national Freeze conference—the official kickoff of the Freeze Campaign. After much debate, the first Freeze strategy paper was approved. It said: "If the world as we know it is to survive, we must pull back immediately from the imminent danger of nuclear annihilation." The strategy paper identified four phases to the campaign:

1. Demonstrate the potential of the Freeze
2. Build broad and visible public support
3. Focus that support on policy makers and create a major national debate
4. Win the debate and make the Freeze a national policy objective

In short: "Let the freeze build and strengthen at the grassroots level and when it has sufficient strength, turn to Washington and bring overwhelming citizen pressure to bear on elected representatives."[2]

In November 1981, Randy Kehler led organizers who placed the freeze resolution on the ballot as a referendum question in three state senate districts in western Massachusetts. It passed 59–41 percent. That displayed the great potential organizing power of the Freeze. In December, the National Clearinghouse for the Nuclear Weapons Freeze Campaign opened in St. Louis. As soon as the phones were in, people started calling and asking how to organize a Freeze group in their town. The staff of the National Clearinghouse couldn't keep up with the Freeze groups as they popped up around the country. The middle-class churches and peace and justice groups, with their access to money, people, media, and politicians, helped to provide the grassroots organizing with a quick start. They solicited endorsements from community leaders, created resolutions of support, gathered signatures on petitions to place proposals on the ballot, and passed state and local resolutions—providing visibility and a strong base for the Freeze.

Freeze Fact Sheet #1, put out by the National Clearinghouse in St. Louis in early 1983, said:

> In two years the campaign won the support of millions of people. In 1982 over 11 million Americans—60% of those voting on the issue—supported the Freeze in state and local referenda around the country. It was the largest referendum in American history. The Freeze has been officially endorsed by 11 state legislatures, 321 City Councils, 444 New England Town Meetings, 61 County Councils, 140 Catholic Bishops, 10 National Labor Unions, (and) 109 National and International Organizations, including the General Assembly of the United Nations.

The Freeze Language as the Frame for the Grassroots Strategy

Freeze grassroots strategy was based on the public appeal of a *commonsense, simple idea* at a time when people were hungry for a way to stop the insanity and anxiety of the nuclear arms race. It was broad, comprehensive, explicitly bilateral, and verifiable. It was conservative and yet dramatic. It gave people an opportunity to act locally and take meaningful action on an issue that had previously seemed completely out of their control. It was good policy and a great grassroots organizing tool—a rare opportunity to bypass the frustrations of interest-group politics and the power of money.

The bilateral nature of the Freeze was calculated to break down old Cold War, anti-Soviet instincts. It provided a Teflon resistance to the previously successful conservative strategy of labeling the peace movement as "communist inspired." It won converts well beyond the peace constituency, both in Congress and around the country. It framed a proposal to appeal to a broad popular grassroots base with the goal of winning a majority of Americans. And it worked. It sits as an example that still needs to be heeded by progressive activists who too often speak primarily "to the choir."

The rank and file speak out at a Nuclear Weapons Freeze Campaign national conference, Chicago, mid-1980s *(records of SANE, Swarthmore College Peace Collection).*

But from the beginning, there were tensions between those who
wanted a narrow focus on a bilateral Freeze because of its popular appeal, and those who felt we needed to confront dangerous individual
weapons systems and U.S. foreign policy. Upon reflection, Kehler would
have pushed harder on confronting individual weapons systems. He
believes we could have begun a campaign such as "no freeze, no funds."
By not taking on these weapons, he believes, we lost credibility in the
disarmament community.

A Local Focus

"Local organizing" was the mantra of the Freeze. Kehler wrote: "The
Freeze Campaign respects the wisdom and authority of local groups
in determining their own Freeze-related programs and actions, while
at the same time recognizing the need for effective coordination at
the national level. Just as important is our commitment to bottom-up,
democratic decision-making within the National Campaign itself."[3]
Regular meetings of the Freeze National Committee and the annual

Freeze conference involved hundreds of activists from around the country who were involved directly in decisions on strategy. The resulting ownership provided the underpinnings of the people power that helped fuel the grassroots success of the Freeze.

The national staff role was to support local grassroots organizing. The Freeze office was created as a clearinghouse, not a traditional headquarters, and it was intentionally located away from the coasts in St. Louis. The job of the clearinghouse staff was to nurture and support grassroots organizers across the country, assist in sharing ideas and materials, and report the impact of our collective actions to each other and to the media.

But as Freeze success built, congressional leaders pressured the Freeze to refocus its strategy on Capitol Hill. Funders began to demand that the Freeze clearinghouse be moved to the East Coast. Media attention was clearly more difficult to command away from the East Coast. We moved to Washington.

Coalition of Peace and Justice Groups: The Initial Framework

The early grassroots popularity of the Freeze was in part due to a good idea striking at the right time, but it was also fueled by an intentional strategy to use the networks of the founding Freeze groups (the American Friends Service Committee, SANE, Clergy and Laity Concerned, the Fellowship of Reconciliation, Council for a Livable World, Sojourners, and others) as a quick start to begin spreading the Freeze across the country. In an organizing windfall, the Freeze also empowered its groups to advance political agendas and helped them build their capacity.

Even so, Kehler raised an important issue about the movement. Writing in June 1984, he observed that we "have scarcely begun to realize the incredible potential that we have for stopping the nuclear arms race.... Realizing the potential that we have, however, is going to require a far greater level of unity and collaboration than perhaps we have ever thought about." He had a

> growing sense that we cannot continue working separately, each within our own institution or organization. We are not, in fact, a disarmament movement. We are a collection of disarmament organizations.... We

need a comprehensive plan for stopping and reversing the nuclear arms race, a plan that not only shows the strategy by which we intend to do this, but a plan that also shows how the efforts of particular organizations fit coherently and cohesively into the overall picture.[4]

Building a National Network of Local Freeze Groups

From 1981 through early 1983, the Freeze grassroots network grew at a dizzying rate. It was like someone lighting a match on a dry prairie. In June 1984, the Freeze staff evaluated its strength: "There is at least some organized Freeze activity in every single state in the country and between 1,000 and 2,000 local groups organizing around the Freeze coast to coast. All this in just three short years since the Freeze Campaign was launched in March of 1981 at Georgetown University." The nuclear freeze was "a major election year issue, with seven of the eight Democratic presidential contenders publicly endorsing it. This is surely an indication of progress. Another indication is a recent public opinion poll commissioned by the right-wing Committee on the Present Danger that revealed that almost everyone had indeed heard of the Freeze and that nearly 80% approved of it."[5]

So why didn't we keep our focus on what we were doing so well—base building at the local level? Why turn to Capitol Hill now? In part, Freeze leaders were afraid the organizing was running out of gas at the local level. They were running out of ideas for outreach projects, racking their brains for new ways to continue to keep the organizing local. Allies in Congress were anxious to begin pushing Freeze proposals. These allies began to assert themselves. They wanted center stage either because of their desire to change policy or because of the potential for building political capital on the back of a very popular movement.

When we moved the focus to Washington, D.C., congressional leaders and staff took control and local supporters became less engaged. Passing a bill became the measure of success instead of how many signatures we gathered or city councils had endorsed the Freeze. We tried to bridge the gap by using the previously successful outreach device of gathering signatures to be delivered during lobby day in Washington and by having people lobby their representatives locally, but the involvement fell off. Despite the appearance of large numbers at lobby days, it represented a relatively small percentage of our supporters.

This raises fascinating questions. Had the Freeze exhausted the attention that any short-term campaign can expect to get from the media and the public? Were there strategies that could have been employed to continue building the Freeze's local base? Randy Kehler believes that a direct action strategy might have helped sustain the passion and local focus. It might have alienated mainstream supporters and fueled concerns that the Freeze was really a radical campaign, but it would have maintained the fire in the belly that we lost when we ran out of local organizing steam and the focus moved to D.C. Randy now believes that we could have sustained both tracks. He concludes, "I would have pushed harder on civil disobedience."

Outreach and Targeting

Between 1981 and 1983, the Freeze had broad support across the country. The list of groups that endorsed the Freeze was long and impressive. This lent important credibility to the campaign at an early stage. But when the time came to convert those endorsements to political power (money and people), few groups beyond the disarmament community were willing to make the Freeze a priority.

Part of the fault was our own. Our approach to labor unions, religious groups, environmental organizations, people of color, and others was based on a campaign called "Make the Freeze the Issue." But as Randy Kehler concluded, "We never got traction" with some of our outreach efforts. A labor leader in St. Louis told me that when he saw peace activists coming, he learned to avoid the meeting because he knew it would be a one-way conversation. The topic would be: "What can you do to help pass a Freeze?" The question should have been: "How can we help each other? Where is our mutual interest?"

The Freeze support built so fast and so overwhelmingly that we were all doing our best to keep our heads above water. That made it difficult to build lasting political relationships. And our narrow strategy of focusing exclusively on the Freeze made it difficult to have the broader two-way conversations that might have yielded stronger, more complex connections. Could we have talked social justice with civil rights groups? Could we have discussed living-wage issues with unions? Our inability to connect with their core issues made it less likely that they would make the Freeze a priority when we needed them.

What could we have done to build a more enduring movement?

Early in the campaign, we had very good, well-documented educational materials detailing the size of the nuclear arsenals, the individual weapons systems, mutually assured destruction, first-strike capability, "use it or lose it" theories, NATO deployment strategies, and other issues. Our early approach at house meetings was to spread out maps of a community overlaid with circles indicating which families would be killed instantly, which would be killed within a few hours, and which later by lingering radiation sickness. Once people found their home, the escalating arms race was no longer a distant government policy.

As the Freeze Campaign evolved, concern developed that fear tactics would only get us so far and we needed to connect with issues of financial security that would provide a longer-term, substantial organizing relationship. The cost of one MX missile would build so many schools or hospitals, would provide housing for so many homeless, and so on. The intention was to make the cost of the nuclear arms race more real to more people.

Frank Blechman, a national organizer for the Freeze, has argued that we would have been better served by continuing to use the more personal approach as our primary outreach and education tool. Historically, many of our largest movements have been built on rights issues that people feel so personally about that they are willing to sacrifice for them: the women's movement, the labor movement, the civil rights movement. They raised basic-survival, bread-and-butter issues: equality, a living wage, prejudice in housing and employment, a healthy workplace—all issues that motivate those affected to stay involved and sacrifice.

Kehler met with a State Department official who said the Reagan administration wasn't worried: The protesters would march and protest loudly over the weekend and then return to their comfortable lives. The official reasoned that he just had to survive the weekend and everything would calm down.

Was the Freeze too abstract and not an issue that impacted people's everyday lives? Could the Freeze have been framed in a more personal way? Blechman believes that we were very successful, at first, in convincing many Americans that they could not live with the escalating number of nuclear weapons, but we did not address the question of people's insecurity in a scary world. Could we have addressed people's gut-level need to "feel secure"?

Lesson for Future Campaigns:
Framing a Broader Vision

To build a stronger, more permanent grassroots base for future campaigns, we need to frame the peace issue in a way that has a personal appeal; has a vision that can help tie together a broad, diverse, and thus powerful coalition; and has the potential to build a majority movement.

Conservatives sell their vision: "Lower taxes, smaller government, and a stronger, more secure America." It is simple, clear, and powerful—like the Freeze. But unlike the Freeze, and unlike progressives in general, that vision has the intention and potential to reach out on a personal level and build powerful coalitions and a majority movement in this country. They move seamlessly from issue to issue, even if their policies are not always consistent with that vision.

By contrast, progressives have built a series of issue groupings that feel like isolated silos with no connection to one another. When asked what we stand for, we recite a litany: health care for all, housing for the homeless, quality education for every American, campaign finance reform, renewable energy, mass transit, and so on. All are very good things, but we have not painted a picture of the world as we would like to see it. And that's the stuff that motivates most people. So, by the time we have finished the list, we have lost most of the audience except the true believers. And there is no connecting vision to build a strong, united grassroots base on behalf of the issues we care about or in support of the candidates who might advance those issues.

A long-term, connecting vision takes extensive thought, conversation, and agreement. That's not an easy task. In the case of the Freeze, those conversations were difficult, and ultimately we agreed only on the narrow language of the Freeze.

What kind of vision might have connected us then, and might connect us now? Another Freeze leader, Pam Solo, advocates rebuilding a peace movement based on common security. "The fundamental lesson of the nuclear age," she argues, "is that no nation can achieve security unilaterally."[6]

As a local example, in St. Louis, a group of Muslims, Christians, and Jews (www.allgodspeople.us) has an educational campaign rooted in the Koran, the Bible, and the Talmud, asking people to redefine what makes them secure. Is it building stronger locks, borders, guns, and pre-emptive attacks, or is it understanding that "I will be more secure only when you are more secure?" The group's campaign theme is: "We are all God's People.... No Exceptions."

Lessons for Future Campaigns: Organizing Versus Mobilizing

The Freeze campaign was very good at involving people in gathering signatures, building endorsement lists, holding fund-raisers, and participating in rallies and marches. But Richard Healey suggests that we did not do as good a job of building long-term relationships with people and organizations. We did not build connections and infrastructure that would allow us to involve people and organizations over a period of time. We *mobilized* people but didn't *organize* them.

But Richard Healey, Dianne Russell, Pat McCullough, and Glen Stassen have described how in some places it did happen. Perhaps the lesson is that we needed an intentional two-part strategy with the Freeze as the bilateral, popular entry point for new activists and a coalition laying the groundwork for a more sustainable, long-term movement by building deep relationships with ongoing organizations.

Maintaining a Long-Term View amid the Chaos of Short-Term Campaigns

Perhaps most important, how do we recognize the opportunity to plant the seeds of long-term change and movement building in the midst of the chaos and urgency of campaigns? Who carries that understanding and perspective?

Most foundations do not have a commitment to build the long-term organizational capacity of their grantees. They don't encourage grantees to develop long-range strategic plans, expand their working partnerships, think about sources of future leadership, or create fund-raising diversity that leads to self-sufficiency. Is there leadership to create this kind of change within the community of funders? How about consulting and training groups or think tanks? Can they become more effective evangelists for teaching organizations to balance short-term campaigns and long-term change strategies?

I have a good friend who ran a successful business. To make sure that he didn't lose his long-term perspective in the intensity of day-to-day work, he created an advisory committee of retired CEOs and met with them twice a year to review his business plan. Perhaps we need to find some way to empower the grizzled veterans of our movement.

Notes

1. In preparation for this article, Ben Senturia interviewed activists/colleagues/friends who were involved in one way or another with the Freeze grassroots strategy: Randy Kehler (executive director of the Freeze), David Cortright (executive director of SANE), Barbara Roche (deputy director of the Freeze), Pam McIntyre (education and outreach coordinator of the Freeze), Frank Blechman (national organizer for the Freeze), Richard Healey (executive director of the Coalition for a New Foreign and Military Policy), Glen Stassen (co-chair of the Freeze Strategy Committee), Dianne Russell (national field organizer for SANE), Rob Kleidman (volunteer for the Wisconsin Freeze). He also gleaned from the following sources: Randy Kehler, Draft Strategy Paper and cover note (Feb. 9, 1981); Randy Kehler, "Message from the National Coordinator" (December 1983); Randy Kehler, "Antiwar Means Pro-Democracy," *Nation* (Oct. 1990); Pam Solo, Institute for a Civil Society (www.civilsocietyinstitute.org); Richard Healey, Grassroots Policy Project (www.grassrootspolicy.org).

2. Randy Kehler, "The Freeze, Three Years After," *Fellowship,* July/Aug. 1984.

3. Ibid.

4. Randy Kehler, "We Need A Common Voice," *Nuclear Times,* June 1984.

5. "The Freeze, Three Years After."

6. Pam Solo, *From Protest to Policy* (New York: Ballinger, 1988).

Chapter 8

"Blessed are the Peacemakers"

People of Faith and the Freeze

Jim Wallis and Jim Rice

From its very beginning (and before), people of faith played a key role in the Nuclear Weapons Freeze Campaign. At all levels—from the leadership to the grassroots—religious people provided a central element in the freeze movement and in the broader peace movement of which it was a part.

The origins of the Freeze Campaign itself illustrate the centrality of religious believers to these efforts. Long before the drafting of the "Call to Halt the Nuclear Arms Race," the precedents for what became the Freeze were already deeply rooted in the faith community.

Pre-Freeze Calls to Halt

The Partial Test Ban Treaty of 1963 sent much of the organizing energy of the antinuclear weapons movement underground (as it did the nuclear tests themselves), and for much of the rest of the decade peace organizing was primarily focused on ending the U.S. war in Vietnam. But the nuclear arms race heated up in the 1970s, and by the middle of the decade the peace movement (and the overlapping movement against nuclear power) began to turn its attention back to nuclear weapons. While large-scale demonstrations were organized at nuclear power plants—such as the April 1977 occupation of the Seabrook plant by 2,000 protesters—efforts aimed at nuclear weapons in this period tended to be much smaller, and decidedly religious, such as the December 1976 arrest of 29 antinuclear protesters at the Pentagon, led by Elizabeth McAlister and others who had founded the Jonah House resistance community (and who engaged in subsequent "Plowshares" actions to symbolically disarm nuclear weapons).

Sojourners magazine published its first special issue on nuclear weapons in February 1977, with the cover prominently proclaiming, "About 35 countries will be able to make atomic weapons within nine years . . . and nuclear war will become inevitable." In the issue, *Sojourners* associate editor Wes Michaelson laid out the essential argument for what later became the Freeze. "In his inaugural address, Jimmy Carter said his 'ultimate goal [was] the elimination of all nuclear weapons from this earth,'" Michaelson wrote. "It is difficult to think of a more concrete way to begin than by simply halting the daily production of additional nuclear bombs." (Michaelson, now Granberg-Michaelson, is currently general secretary of the Reformed Church in America.) The *Sojourners* special issue also included Fr. Richard McSorley's noted essay titled "It's a Sin to Build a Nuclear Weapon."

The special nuclear weapons edition of the magazine was only the opening foray in what became a full-scale national campaign organized by Sojourners. The next year, Sojourners produced "The Nuclear Challenge to Christian Conscience: A Study Guide for Churches," issued in conjunction with the first U.N. Special Session on Disarmament, and distributed 25,000 copies in the succeeding months. Included in the packet was "A Call to Faithfulness," a Christian statement calling for a "suspension" of all nuclear weapons tests and all plans for new strategic weapons systems, and a repudiation of the U.S. "first-use" military doctrine, as "minimal first steps" toward the goal of eliminating nuclear weapons. The statement was signed by hundreds of Christian leaders, from Dan Berrigan, Henri Nouwen, and Dorothy Day to William Stringfellow and John Howard Yoder.

The lead article in the study guide, "A Time to Stop," was written by Richard J. Barnet, a founder of the Institute for Policy Studies and a member of the Church of the Saviour in Washington, D.C. In the article, Barnet decried the escalating nuclear arms race and in particular noted that "the U.S.-Soviet detente has not produced any change on either side in the institutions or habits of mind that keep the arms race going." The arms control process, Barnet wrote, failed to stop the arms race: "While the diplomats haggled at the SALT talks, stockpiles of nuclear weapons on both sides doubled, and major advances in military technology—such as MIRV, MARV, the cruise missile, and the new, more powerful Soviet missiles—were introduced."

Barnet saw a clear way out of the U.S.-Soviet nuclear death spiral: Stop. He wrote:

> The only way to stop the arms race is for both sides to communicate to each other a clear intention to stop, based on the recognition that the risks of moving to a new stage of insanity outweigh the risks of peace.... To break out of that spiral [of the arms race], the United States should take some clear and courageous independent initiatives that will convey our intention to find a new basis for our security.... There are many moves we could make right now to stop the arms race.

Barnet went on to argue the importance of citizen action to bring about this stoppage of the arms race, and in particular the need for the churches to be involved.

> Is it possible for the Christian church to play a prophetic role at this critical moment in human history by launching a massive public education campaign to help the American people to confront the moral bankruptcy of the policies and institutions that are providing them with the illusion of security at the cost of sacrificing their most precious beliefs? Could the church take the lead in organizing mayors and city officials, union people, congresspersons, and citizens from communities across the country to press the president to make an historic initiative for peace?

The first national organizing efforts in support of this approach—"the way to stop is to stop"—came in 1979. In June of that year, President Jimmy Carter and Soviet General Secretary Leonid Brezhnev signed the SALT II agreement in Vienna, Austria, setting even-higher levels of strategic offensive weapons in the arsenals of the two superpowers. The U.S. peace movement was torn: Many peace organizations felt compelled to support the SALT treaty, feeling it was the best agreement possible in the context of the Cold War. But many in the religious community, and others, felt that the treaty merely codified the continued escalation of the arms race. Sojourners' Jim Wallis and Wes Michaelson—who had been an assistant to Sen. Mark Hatfield (R–OR) in foreign affairs and defense policy—drafted a "moratorium" amendment to the SALT treaty, which Hatfield, an evangelical Christian, introduced in the Senate in June. The amendment, as Sen. Hatfield explained in a September 1979 "dear colleague" letter to fellow senators, would "freeze the strategic nuclear arsenals of both the Soviet Union and the United States at their present levels—a nuclear moratorium." The amendment, Hatfield continued, would "freeze 'further development, testing, and deployment' of those strategic nuclear systems which are now in place, and prohibit the introduction of any new strategic nuclear systems." In testimony before the Senate Foreign Relations Committee that same month, Hatfield argued that the amendment would "freeze the strategic arms race; it would stop escalation by simply halting it." The Hatfield freeze amendment became the focus of national organizing for Sojourners and other religious organizations for the next two years; these efforts were combined with other peace organizing work when the Freeze went national in March 1981.

The Freeze Campaign

In the summer of 1979, Randall Forsberg made her freeze proposal at a Mobilization for Survival conference in Louisville, Kentucky. In fall 1979, Wallis and Mernie King, director of Sojourners Peace Ministry, traveled to western Massachusetts to discuss the nuclear moratorium with Randy Kehler and others at the Traprock Peace Center. Traprock, the western Massachusetts branch of the American Friends Service Committee, and others, organized referenda on the issue throughout the western part of the state. The nonbinding moratorium referenda were eventually approved by voters in 59 of the 62 Massachusetts towns where it was on the ballot. (See chapter 7.)

Later in 1979, Sojourners called for grassroots actions at legislative offices across the country in support of the moratorium. In response, local church-based activists organized demonstrations on December 3 in 63 cities and towns, including a gathering on the steps of the U.S. Capitol. Weeks later, the Soviet Union invaded Afghanistan, and the SALT treaty was withdrawn from consideration in the Senate.

But education and organizing in support of what was becoming known as the Freeze continued to grow, and churches continued to be front and center. In its August 1979 issue, *Sojourners* ran an interview with evangelist Billy Graham, who spoke of his "change of heart" on the arms race, saying, "The present arms race is a terrifying thing, and it is almost impossible to overestimate its potential for disaster.... Is a nuclear holocaust inevitable if the arms race is not stopped? Frankly, the answer is almost certainly yes."

By early 1980, five national religious peace organizations—all of which had opposed the SALT treaty as inadequate and supported an immediate arms halt along the lines of the Hatfield amendment—began a coordinated effort to bring the issue of the nuclear arms race and a nuclear moratorium before the churches as a spiritual and moral issue. The groups—which included Sojourners, the Fellowship of Reconciliation (FOR), Pax Christi, World Peacemakers, and New Call to Peacemaking, and later the Southern Christian Leadership Conference—stressed the importance, not only of political organizing on behalf of the moratorium, but also of grounding the work on moral and religious foundations. The initial meeting included "a repeated call for clear linking of renewal of the spiritual life and the call to nuclear moratorium," wrote John Stoner of New Call to Peacemaking, a cooperative effort of the Church of the Brethren, Friends, and Mennonites.

The six groups eventually solidified around a document titled "The New Abolitionist Covenant," which called for a freeze as a "first step toward abolishing nuclear weapons altogether." The document argued that "the nuclear threat is not just a political issue any more than slavery was: It is a question that challenges our worship of God and our commitment to Jesus Christ. In other words, the growing prospect of nuclear war presents us with more than a test of survival; it confronts us with a test of faith." (The groups also produced an interfaith version of the Covenant.) In its first year, more than one million copies of the Covenant were ordered, printed, and distributed. The "covenant groups" continued to collaborate for the next decade, working to deepen support in their various constituencies and in the church at large for the Freeze and other peacemaking efforts.

Needless to say, other religious organizations and people of faith of all stripes were involved in the many pre-Freeze Campaign peace activities, from large demonstrations—such as the gathering of 16,000 in May 1978 to mark the opening of the U.N. Special Session on Disarmament—to smaller conferences and seminars, such as the May 1980 consultation convened by the National Council of Churches in support of the moratorium.

In 1980, as momentum coalesced around the Call to Halt the Nuclear Arms Race, much of the work in preparation for the initial Freeze national conference was done by religious peace organizations, in particular Clergy and Laity Concerned, FOR, and the American Friends Service Committee. These national religious organizations approached the Center for Peace Studies, a small peace center founded and directed by Fr. Richard McSorley at one of the nation's preeminent Jesuit institutions, Georgetown University in Washington, D.C. As a campus-based organization, the center was able to offer use of campus facilities for the initial Freeze national conference in March 1981 at student rates—a very important consideration for the budget-conscious organizers of the early days of the Freeze.

Following the national conference at Georgetown, education and mobilization began in every constituency represented—from labor unions to business people, and from teachers to members of Congress—and the religious community was at the forefront of much of that work. Sojourners and other national organizations targeted the churches in particular. For instance, early in 1981 Sojourners published a 108-page study guide for churches on the nuclear arms race, titled "A Matter of Faith," of which almost 100,000 copies were distributed. The following year, Sojourners founder Jim Wallis edited *Waging Peace: A Handbook for the Struggle to Abolish Nuclear Weapons* (Harper & Row), which included a section titled "Freezing the Arms Race: The First Step Toward Disarmament."

The Institutional Faith Organizations Engage

By 1983, the institutional churches had joined the debate that the Freeze campaign had raised, and they did so in a big way. The most prominent were the U.S. Catholic Bishops, whose seminal 1983 pastoral letter *The Challenge of Peace: God's Promise and Our Response* shaped the whole discourse, in churches and in society at large, around the moral dimensions of war and peace. "Catholic teaching on peace and war," the bishops wrote, "has had two purposes: to help Catholics form their consciences and to contribute to the public policy debate about the morality of war...."

The wider civil community, although it does not share the same vision of faith, is equally bound by certain key moral principles." In particular, the bishops offered "support for immediate, bilateral, verifiable agreements to halt the testing, production, and deployment of new nuclear weapons systems."

Catholics and Jews supported the Freeze with larger percentages than did Protestants. For example, "in May 1983, when the Catholic bishops adopted their pastoral letter, polls reported that 82 percent of Jews, 78 percent of Catholics, and 57 percent of Protestants supported a Nuclear Freeze."[1] Lawrence Wittner reports:

> Among Jewish groups, the Conservative Rabbinical Assembly of America endorsed the Freeze, as did its Reform counterpart, the Union of American Hebrew Congregations (UAHC), which also demanded a 50 percent cut in nuclear stockpiles. In February 1983, the Synagogue Council of America, a loose umbrella group for all branches of Judaism, called upon Reagan and Andropov "to implement a bilateral mutual cessation of the production and deployment of nuclear weapons." Rabbi Alexander Schindler, president of the UAHC, declared that the nuclear arms race was the "central moral issue of our day."[2]

Virtually every major Christian denomination in the country, and most faith groups, produced statements and engaged in education and action on behalf of peace in the years around the launching of the Freeze, and these became important platforms for people of faith. In 1978, 1979, and 1980, the Southern Baptist Convention passed resolutions calling for peacemaking and "multilateral arms control as an essential ingredient in peacemaking," and for repentance for not having done enough for peacemaking; and *The Baptist Peacemaker* began its publication—which continues today. The United Presbyterian Church in the USA produced *Peacemaking: The Believer's Calling* in 1980, which declared that "peacemaking is an indispensable ingredient of the church's mission. It is not peripheral or secondary but essential to the church's faithfulness to Christ in our time."[3] The United Church of Christ in 1985 declared itself a "just peace" church and published *A Just Peace Church.*[4] And the United Methodist Council of Bishops went perhaps the farthest in its 1986 document *In Defense of Creation,* stating: "Therefore, we say a clear and unconditional No to nuclear war and to any use of nuclear weapons. We conclude that nuclear deterrence is a position that cannot receive the church's blessing." We support a "comprehensive test ban to inaugurate a nuclear freeze."[5] In 1991, the historic peace churches (Mennonite,

Friends, and Brethren) joined together in producing *A Declaration on Peace: In God's People the World's Renewal Has Begun.*[6]

Only within evangelical and Fundamentalist ranks did substantial religious opposition emerge to the Freeze Campaign. In response to an official invitation, President Reagan gave his "evil empire" speech to a meeting of the National Association of Evangelicals in an effort to mobilize evangelicals against the Freeze. Fundamentalists like Jerry Falwell and the Moral Majority conspired with Reagan on ways to oppose the Freeze, and they used their very substantial communications and financial resources to attack the Freeze as what they said was part of a Communist conspiracy to conquer the United States. Falwell published a booklet attacking the Freeze. It quoted a militaristic organization, the American Security Council (surely so named to sound, misleadingly, like the government's National Security Council), as the source for its arguments, rather than the Bible. Lawrence Wittner reports:

> In a lengthy fundraising letter of June 17, 1982, Falwell promised "a major campaign" against "the freeze-niks" ... Starting in the spring of 1983, Falwell placed full-page newspaper ads in the *Washington Post, New York Times,* and more than 70 other newspapers, denouncing "the freeze-niks" ... and exhorting "patriotic, God-fearing Americans to speak up" for military defense.... On March 20, 1983, he told listeners: "This idea of unilateral disarmament is nothing more than slavery for our children."[7]

But the efforts of the major denominations, and similar activities in almost all faith communities, resulted in an outpouring of action on behalf of the Freeze and other peace initiatives in churches, synagogues, temples, and everywhere else people of faith gathered, and the Freeze grew even stronger in the polls. For many of these people, working for the Freeze as a first step toward abolishing nuclear weapons—and even war itself—was not merely a political act but a matter of faith itself, based on the firm belief, as Scripture puts it: "Blessed are the peacemakers, for they shall be called children of God."

Notes

1. Lawrence S. Wittner, *Toward Nuclear Abolition: A History of the World Nuclear Disarmament Movement, 1971 to the Present* (Stanford: Stanford University Press, 2003), p. 181.

2. Ibid., p. 180.

3. United Presbyterian Church in the U.S.A., *Peacemaking: The Believer's Calling* (New York: General Assembly of the United Presbyterian Church in the U.S.A., 1980).

4. Susan Thistlethwaite, ed., *A Just Peace Church* (New York: United Church Press, 1996).

5. United Methodist Council of Bishops, *In Defense of Creation* (Nashville: Graded Press, 1986).

6. Douglas Gwyn, George Hunsinger, Eugene F. Roop, and John Howard Yoder, *A Declaration on Peace: In God's People the World's Renewal Has Begun* (Scottdale, PA: Herald Press, 1991).

7. Wittner, p. 190.

Chapter 9

Women in the Antinuclear Movement

Monica Green

> I suddenly learned what every mother must learn: That I would die to save the lives of my children, and that if they weren't going to survive, nothing else I ever did would matter. At that moment, I accepted personal responsibility for stopping the nuclear arms race.
>
> *Helen Caldicott*

One summer in Maine, when I was a teenager, I found Nevil Shute's 1957 novel *On the Beach* on my parents' bookshelves and quickly became engrossed in the wrenching story of the impact of nuclear war on the residents of Melbourne. The fact that my family was Australian amplified the book's effect on my young mind. It is to my reading of this fictitious account of nuclear warfare that I trace my earliest awareness of nuclear weaponry and its consequences.

A few years later, I was finishing college at Oberlin where students were beginning to talk about the Nuclear Weapons Freeze proposal. Although I participated in efforts to organize resistance to President Reagan's reinstatement of registration for the draft, my campus activism was focused on reproductive health, and I pursued that field professionally after graduating in 1981. Before moving to Cleveland to work at a women's health clinic, however, I attended a program marking the anniversary of the bombings of Hiroshima and Nagasaki. A photojournalist reported on her visit to Japan and recounted interviews with survivors of the atomic bombings. These images of human suffering and cultural devastation contrasted sharply with Reagan's casual rhetoric about waging and winning nuclear war. I grew increasingly concerned about the direction of U.S. policy.

In early 1983 I joined hundreds of people in a large crowded church in Cleveland Heights to hear Dr. Helen Caldicott lecture about nuclear weapons. Caldicott, a pediatrician, was and still is one of the most visible women in the antinuclear movement. Born in 1938 in Melbourne, Australia, Caldicott was also influenced by *On the Beach,* and during the 1960s launched a successful campaign to halt French atmospheric nuclear testing in the Pacific Ocean. Caldicott came to the United States in 1977 to teach and practice medicine, but within five years she had left Harvard and Boston Children's Hospital to tour and speak full time for the antinuclear movement. Caldicott's passion, combined with her medical expertise, made her an extremely effective spokesperson, and she helped generate a groundswell of grassroots antinuclear activism in the early 1980s.

In addition to reviving Physicians for Social Responsibility in the United States, Caldicott helped start similar organizations in other countries. In 1980 she founded the Women's Party for Survival, which soon became known as Women's Action for Nuclear Disarmament. WAND played a leading role in opposing the Reagan administration's military buildup. During the 1990s, WAND, which changed its name in 1991 to Women's Action for New Directions, expanded its focus to broader issues of world peace and security, as well as redirection of military spending toward human and environmental needs. The organization has remained a vital vehicle for women activists, especially since the inauguration of WiLL, the Women Legislators' Lobby, a nonpartisan network of women state legislators who coordinate efforts to influence federal policy. STAND, Students Taking Action for New Directions, founded in 1999 by young WAND activists, works to engage the next generation of women in peace issues. When I first heard Caldicott speak in 1983, I was stunned by both her words and slides. Nothing I had read or seen previously about nuclear war had affected me as profoundly. In the weeks that followed, I experienced a deep sense of hopelessness about the fate of the world under the influence of a belligerent U.S. president. I wrote letters to my dearest college friends expressing fears that our lives would be cut short by nuclear war, and consoled myself with the thought that I was fortunate to have had 23 years on this earth.

It took several phone calls from Freeze organizers to penetrate my despair. I had signed various petitions and forms during Caldicott's talk, and fortunately the Cleveland Heights Freeze activists were persistent and continued to call me about meetings and events until I finally showed up at one. Once I met the lively and dedicated group of volunteers who made up the core of the Cleveland Heights Freeze chapter, I was hooked. I traveled to Washington, D.C., to attend the 20th anniversary of Martin Luther King's historic 1963 march. As the months passed, my life began to revolve around my involvement in the Freeze campaign. I tabled at events, attended meetings, phone-banked, helped organize the first fundraising walkathon, and phoned new volunteers. I made new friends whose determination to effect change through the political process gave me hope about the future. A year later, following the reelection of President Reagan, I left my job at the clinic to work full time for nuclear disarmament as executive director of the Greater Cleveland Freeze Campaign.

The Cleveland Freeze office was located on the second floor of an old brick building with large windows facing downtown Cleveland just across the Cuyahoga River. To this office each day came one or more of a loyal group of volunteers: Roni Berenson, Rae Epstein, Roma Foldy, and Annie Heller. These women, whose time was no longer claimed by children or professional responsibilities, also served on the board and were active in local chapters. Like similar volunteers across the country during this period, they kept our busy office humming: answering the phone, supervising mailings, processing contributions, managing our first computerized donor database, photocopying, scheduling meetings, and much, much more. The commitment of these women to managing the office, with the support of many other volunteers, allowed our small paid staff to focus on building an organization capable of exerting political pressure on our elected officials to change nuclear weapons policy.

The Cleveland board, and its leadership, was fairly balanced among women and men. Daisy Ford served as president during the first year

I was on staff and she remained a mentor to me long after she stepped down from that role. In contrast to the board, however, our office was predominantly female. In addition to a preponderance of female volunteers, over the years we also employed more women than men. This was especially evident during the 1988 election season, when several energetic young women joined our office through the national Freeze Voter effort to channel grassroots peace activism into important senate races.

Randall Forsberg

As I made my way in a new profession as grassroots organizer, I was inspired by a host of women. One was Randall Forsberg, often referred to as "the mother of the Freeze." I had heard Forsberg address national Freeze conferences and was thrilled to meet her when she came to Cleveland to speak. As a novice young woman activist, I found Forsberg's words of encouragement invaluable. They boosted my confidence as I became more deeply involved in the movement.

As a defense analyst, Forsberg stood out in a field dominated by men. I had joined the Freeze movement out of concern for the future of our planet; I was appalled by the horror nuclear weapons had wrought in Hiroshima and Nagasaki. Once I got involved, I quickly learned that the nuclear policy debate was full of technicalities. Without a background in science or military policy, I found keeping up with all the weapons' acronyms, much less understanding the intricacies of nuclear physics, a serious challenge. Every time I heard Forsberg speak about weapons and defense policy, she made complex issues accessible. This was part of what made her "Call to Halt the Nuclear Arms Race" brilliant: it cut through the technical jargon and advocated a mutual, verifiable halt to the nuclear arms race in language that laypeople could easily grasp. She wrote the "Call" after giving a speech to a conference in Louisville, Kentucky; her experience as a schoolteacher no doubt contributed to her ability to help citizens make sense of technical defense matters.

Had I known as a young activist what I have since learned about Randall Forsberg, I would have been even more inspired. A native of Alabama and graduate of Barnard College, Forsberg began her career in disarmament in 1968 as a typist at the Stockholm International Peace Research Institute (SIPRI) before becoming an editor and researcher there. Subsequently she studied defense at the Massachusetts Institute of Technology, and in 1980 she founded the Institute for Defense and

Randy Forsberg, defense and disarmament expert and founder of the Nuclear Weapons Freeze Campaign, 1982 (*records of SANE, Swarthmore College Peace Collection*).

Disarmament Studies (IDDS). Forsberg received a MacArthur Foundation Fellows award in 1983; in 1995 President Clinton appointed her to the expert advisory board to the U.S. Arms Control and Disarmament Agency. Forsberg has authored many books and articles and since 1982 IDDS has published the monthly *Arms Control Reporter* as well as the annual World Arms Database. She speaks extensively and, in addition to addressing public policy critics, has briefed high-level government officials, testified before the U.S. Congress, and spoken at West Point, the U.S. Air Force Academy, the National Defense University, and the German War College. It is a testament to Forsberg's unique skills and leadership abilities that she has succeeded in bridging the two distinct worlds of disarmament advocacy and the military establishment.

Helen Seidman, Ohio's Robin Hood

As the new director of the Greater Cleveland Freeze, I soon attended a meeting of the Ohio Nuclear Weapons Freeze. Statewide coordinating meetings were held on Saturdays in Columbus, a two-and-a-half-hour drive from Cleveland. It was Helen Seidman who persuaded me of the importance of strengthening the statewide effort. Seidman, who lived in Lake County just east of the Cleveland metropolitan area, was essentially a full-time volunteer for the Freeze. When I met her in 1984, Helen had been traveling around Ohio with John Looney, director of the Northeast Ohio American Friends Service Committee, starting peace groups in each of the state's 88 counties. Looney was called by some a "Johnny Appleseed for peace and non-violence"; Seidman initiated "the Robin Hood approach" to peace organizing in Ohio. In the mid-1980s, Ohio had twenty-one congressional seats. Fewer than half of these were held by supporters of the Freeze, and seven of those supporters were concentrated in the populous northeast corner of the state. Helen's philosophy was that the human and financial resources of our progressive region needed to be liberally shared with more conservative parts of Ohio in order to raise awareness of the nuclear arms race and generate political support for the Freeze.

In 1986 I helped persuade Helen to succeed John Looney as president of the Ohio Freeze, partly by agreeing to serve, with Linda Musmeci Kimball, as a vice president of the state organization.[1] Helen was a tireless, dynamic leader who always asked thoughtful questions, listened carefully to the answers, and followed up on *everything*. After laying the groundwork throughout Ohio for a network of grassroots activism, Helen next worked to expand the peace movement's media savvy so as to increase exposure of our positions in the news media. Helen sparkled with a love of life that motivated her peace work, and her joy was contagious. The peace movement lost a beloved grassroots leader when, in 1995, Helen died while vacationing in Florida with her husband when a speeding vehicle hit the bicycle she was riding.

Uniting with SANE

My attendance at two national Freeze conferences had exposed me to the diverse network of grassroots chapters across the country, as well as to the national leadership—both staff and board—of the movement. Interested in learning more, and seeing how our work in Ohio fit into the national effort, I volunteered to represent the Ohio affiliate at a National Committee meeting of the Freeze. I became friends with Kye Briesath, who directed the Maryland state affiliate. We were about the same age, although Kye had much more experience as a community organizer, and we shared a deep commitment to grassroots activism as a strategy for social change. When seats opened on the national executive committee of the Freeze, both of us ran and were elected.

The National Committee of the Freeze was committed to diversity of representation and adopted several policies to ensure equal inclusion of women in the national leadership. If affiliates elected a male representative to the national board, they were required to elect a female alternate. If there was a gender imbalance on the National Committee, lots would be drawn and some affiliates would be asked to seat their female alternates. By policy, at least one of the elected national co-chairs of the committee was a woman.[2]

On the national Freeze staff, Jane Gruenebaum had succeeded Randy Kehler, the first national director. When Jane departed, Dottye Burt-Markowitz, who had been hired to direct membership development, served as acting national director. Carolyn Cottom, a grassroots activist from Tennessee, was selected as the next executive director. Cottom led the Freeze staff during the merger with SANE and then served with David Cortright as co-director of the merged organization. It was clear that there was a strong commitment to inclusion of women on the national staff as well. Beth Grupp, who served as development director,

Monica Green, on the job for the SANE/Freeze national organization, August 1989 *(Monica Green)*.

and Kay Shaw, publications director, were just two of many dedicated women who staffed the national office of the Freeze Campaign.

When discussions about merging with SANE got under way in 1987, I met several women who were influential in both the funding and political spheres. Cora Weiss, president of the Rubin Foundation and a member of the SANE board, was a dynamic organizer with a long history of activism, particularly in Women Strike for Peace (WSP). Cora was instrumental in the merger, as was Meg Gage, director of the Peace Development Fund (PDF). Meg, who helped incubate the Freeze concept at the Traprock Peace Center in western Massachusetts, founded PDF in 1981, directed it until 1992, and has continued to be a progressive and activist voice in the funding community. Finally, when I started attending meetings of the SANE and Freeze Unity Commission, I met Andrea Ayvazian, then on the PDF staff, whose trainings on fundraising, board development, and antiracism were widely attended by grassroots Freeze activists in the mid-1980s, contributing significantly to expanding organizational capacity at the grassroots.

My involvement in the antinuclear movement accelerated quickly in the late 1980s. At the end of 1987 I was elected co-chair of the Freeze National Committee, with another local organizer, Chris Brown. As merger negotiations progressed, I served as co-chair, with Cora Weiss, of the transition team, overseeing the practical details of uniting the Freeze with SANE. In mid-1989 I moved to Washington, D.C., to join the staff of the merged organization as field director. When Nick Carter, the first postmerger executive director, left in August 1990, I became acting director of the national office, and subsequently executive director.

I stepped into this new role during a time fraught with political change. The Berlin Wall had fallen, but the first Gulf War presaged new challenges for the peace movement. While Saddam Hussein's invasion of Kuwait precipitated the largest mobilization of the U.S. peace movement since the early 1980s, that antiwar sentiment proved difficult to sustain. Internally, the organizational repercussions of the SANE/Freeze merger were playing themselves out. The national office was almost half a million dollars in debt, had recently moved to a new location with a lease it could no longer afford, and could not meet payroll. These financial challenges had to be resolved if the organization was to survive to pursue its political mission.

The staff members I worked with during that period were extraordinary. Deeply committed to the mission of Peace Action,[3] they were willing to work hard and creatively and to live within the limitations of low salaries and few benefits as well as periodically delayed paychecks. The feminist managerial style that I had developed in Cleveland was essential during this difficult period. Adopting the philosophy that each person has a voice, that everyone's participation is essential, and that we are all interdependent was the only way our staff could have navigated the painful budget crunch and the many challenges of the early 1990s.

We Have a History

Women who have played key roles during Peace Action's first 50 years follow in the footsteps of many women in this country who have publicly advocated for peace at least since the 19th century. Seasoned peace activists know that the Mother's Day holiday we celebrate every spring has its roots in an antiwar "Mother's Day Proclamation" written in 1870 by Julia Ward Howe. Amy Swerdlow, in her history of Women Strike for Peace, characterizes the early 20th-century efforts as being united in "their belief that war was a gender-linked social evil, caused by male competitiveness, materialism, and violence. Women, they were convinced, would play a decisive role in ending war because world peace could be achieved only if men behaved more like women."[4] During this period there was a significant overlap between women's peace advocacy and the movement for women's right to vote. While some women's peace advocacy efforts emphasized the traditional role of women as nurturers, others focused on the right of women to have a say on issues of war and peace.

The beginning of World War I prompted the founding of the first women's group solely focused on peace, the Women's Peace Party, in 1915. One of its founders, the social worker and reformer Jane Addams, also helped found the Women's International League for Peace and Freedom (WILPF). The following decade, more autonomous women's peace groups were born: the Women's Peace Society, the Women's Peace Union, and the National Committee on the Cause and Cure of War. These and other organizations contributed to the growth of the women's peace constituency, despite red-baiting and other attacks from the political right.

WILPF was the only one of these early women's groups, however, to survive European fascism, World War II, and the McCarthy era. Now more than 90 years old, WILPF remains the only international women's organization devoted to peace and disarmament. For decades, I have followed WILPF's work through the involvement of my mother, Audley Green, who has organized or resuscitated several chapters, served on the national board, and traveled internationally to attend WILPF conferences and network with women peace activists from every corner of the earth.

A new women's peace organization, Women Strike for Peace, was born on November 1, 1961, when thousands of mothers and "housewives" staged a one-day walkout to call for an end to atmospheric nuclear testing. Dagmar Wilson, an active member of the D.C. chapter of SANE, organized the women's strike in part because she was impatient with the predominantly male SANE leadership's response to the revelation that milk was being contaminated by strontium-90, a result of radioactive fallout from nuclear tests. The experience of Wilson and other early women WSP leaders in SANE, which struggled in its earliest years with aggressive red-baiting, led them to adopt a decentralized grassroots organizational structure and to reject formal membership requirements. In addition, women strikers made the most of their image as traditional stay-at-home mothers to convey their concern for the world's children with maternal authority. Broad popular support made WSP a politically powerful organization that helped bring about the Limited Test Ban Treaty in 1963.

Inspired by Our Outrage and Compassion

My experience as a woman in Peace Action and its predecessors has been very much shaped by growing up during the modern women's movement. I never questioned whether I could play an active role in a movement such as the Freeze, and from my earliest involvement I received support and encouragement from both men and women. While I have observed tension, and sometimes conflict, stemming from culturally learned sexism, this has ultimately been overshadowed by the universal commitment of Peace Action activists and leaders to create a more peaceful, just society.

The story I have shared of my own involvement in Peace Action tells of some of the women I have known and respected who made a difference—some locally, some globally. Some of these women inspire others to action with their words, passion, and leadership. Some run organizations, volunteer on boards, or leave lucrative careers to work full time for peace. Others march in protest, lobby elected officials, write letters to the editor, or simply speak up for a peaceful approach to conflicts. Whether motivated by our outrage or our compassion, by our love for our children or of this planet, we all believe that war is not the answer and that we can, and must, do what we are able to create peace in this world.

Notes

1. Linda directed the Oxford Citizens for Peace and Justice in southwestern Ohio.

2. In addition, there was a continuing effort to include people of color in the national leadership of the Freeze. This was more difficult than creating gender balance since the grassroots chapters were overwhelmingly white. The Third World Caucus of the Committee helped recruit at-large representatives to increase our racial diversity. The caucus helped the Freeze reach out to groups working on U.S. policy toward Central America and South Africa, as well as American civil rights issues, and during the merger with SANE it helped move the national organization toward a more complex analysis of U.S. foreign policy.

3. The new name was adopted in 1993.

4. Amy Swerdlow, *Women Strike for Peace: Traditional Motherhood and Radical Politics in the 1960s* (Chicago and London: University of Chicago Press, 1993), pp. 28–29.

Chapter 10

The Founding and Early Years of Peace Action

Andrea Ayvazian

The 1980s brought a new wave of peace movement dynamism, and for some folks who are in their middle years today, those heady times were defining moments in their development as social and political activists. The names of William Sloane Coffin Jr., Helen Caldicott, Cora Weiss, Monica Green, David Cortright, Betsy Taylor, Pam Solo, Randy Kehler, and Randy Forsberg must be added to the long list of movement leaders and luminaries of the past because these women and men provided leadership during an exciting, turbulent, and history-changing decade. These visionary scholars and activists gave the peace movement of the 1980s voice, direction, and stature.

Working Together for the Merger

The 1980s were a time of unrest and high energy, a time when high school and college students, young mothers and fathers, and older adults all joined hands and worked in concert with one another, believing that we could slow or stop the build-up of nuclear weapons and that we could create a thaw in the bitter Cold War. We believed we could effect significant change on a national level. It was an electric time—filled with a sense of hope and possibility.

The two largest and most powerful national peace organizations of the time—SANE and the Freeze Campaign—gave the movement its clearest agenda and offered a sense of cohesion and connection to the grassroots groups that sprang up across the country as excitement about the peace movement grew and spread. These two national groups shared similar goals: stop the production and deployment of nuclear weapons, reduce the growing aggression and fear-mongering of the Cold War, and redirect funding from a swollen military budget to social programs that meet human needs. Both organizations organized marches and rallies, teach-ins and die-ins, town meetings and letter writing campaigns, and opportunities to engage in civil disobedience. Both organizations had national offices with paid staff, a loyal following with grassroots chapters across the country, solid funding from individuals and foundations, trusted advisors from the academic, political, funding, and religious communities, and an ability to mobilize huge numbers of people on fairly short notice. Although both SANE and the Freeze were strong, independent organizations, the leaders of the two groups worried about a sense of redundancy in their plans and initiatives, and fear about competing for limited resources nagged those at the top.

Aware that any social movement thrives when there is a shared sense of unity and purpose and suffers when grassroots activists feel divided, confused, or overwhelmed, a group of key leaders from both SANE and the Freeze Campaign began meeting in Washington, D.C., in 1987 to discuss merging the two organizations. The idea was to discuss combining the visions, staffs, finances, and long-range plans of the two organizations to create one larger and stronger organization. The leaders from SANE and the Freeze met for long and emotional meetings during which the goals of a merged organization were discussed and the details of who/what/where and how were hammered out. Although everyone present was committed to the same overall goals, those present wondered how the new organization would or could retain the

Working together: Carolyn Cottom (executive director, Freeze) and David Cortright (executive director, SANE) arrive at the Iceland summit conference in Reykjavik, October 1986 *(records of SANE, Swarthmore College Peace Collection).*

vital characteristics of SANE and the Freeze. Would one organization dominate the other? Would one organization be subsumed under the other—in reality, if not in theory? Could a new merged organization survive? Could a "hybrid," as the new organization was sometimes called, truly be larger and stronger or would it be a diluted version of the two parent organizations and doomed to failure? During laborious meetings that spanned many months, people were asked to be open and honest, to have faith and suspend judgment, to listen deeply and well, and to hear all points and arguments before responding to any one idea or course of action.

One major question was whether to retain the single political focus of the Freeze as an anti-nuclear organization or to broaden the mission to incorporate a critique of other foreign policy issues such as military intervention in Central America and human rights in South Africa. Michael Klare's writings on low-intensity conflict helped deepen our understanding of the complexities of Cold War politics. Carolyn Cottom helped us examine the ways living in a racist society hindered our clear vision of the world.

Another issue was whether to select a president whose authority was primarily moral, such as Bill Coffin or Bob Edgar, or primarily political. Both brought great talent and were enthusiastic about the opportunity.

Structural issues had to be decided: how much decision-making authority should rest with the grassroots (the role of the National Congress, giving a majority of seats on the board to the affiliate-elected members, and so on), and how to share financial resources between the grassroots and the national organization.[1]

I remember those meetings well, and I am moved even today by the stamina, wisdom, patience, and flexibility that those present demonstrated. The leaders from the two groups who met month after month held on to a vision of what might be the best course of action for the peace movement—not what was in their own self-interest or what might further the agenda of the organization they particularly loved. The long, careful, and thorough process finally came to an end when everyone involved—the leaders of both SANE and the Freeze and their boards of directors and key advisors—put the finishing touches on the plan for a newly merged organization known as "SANE/Freeze." I remember the relief, pride, excitement, and exhaustion at the last meeting when the newly formed, merged organization was being born. Like midwives who had labored with a birth mother for hours (actually weeks and months), we collapsed and cried and cheered when SANE/Freeze was finally born!

When the Cold War ended in 1989, funding from our phone program and foundations dropped off rapidly. Furthermore, SANE's canvass programs—which had enabled the rapid growth of SANE during the early 1980s—were decentralized to affiliates, and their revenues no longer supported the national office. We had to move to a more expensive office from our old space fraught with problems including building code violations, and although we reduced staff dramatically, income reduced faster than staff did. We quickly piled up a debt of $500,000. Monica Green as executive director of SANE/Freeze then did a fantastic job of saving the organization by holding down the budget and leading us in paying off the debt.

Our fears that the new SANE/Freeze would not be a powerful force for change in the national peace movement were unfounded, and the organization, with its funding consolidated from the two parent organizations and a strong staff, new board, and team of advisors, hit the ground running as soon as the announcement was made and the transition from two organizations to one newly-formed, merged organization took place physically.

Part of the reason that SANE/Freeze—later renamed "Peace Action"—was so successful is that as an organization it never lost its connection to the grassroots and it did not become top-heavy or dizzy from the rarified air of Washington D.C. Peace Action was able to maintain a sense of serving the grassroots rather than dominating or trampling them, and it did not succumb to the sense of self-importance that so often befalls organizations based in the country's capital. Instead Peace Action remained light on its feet, responsive and flexible, leading by pushing those in small communities from coast to coast.

The Movement Moment

What remains with me about being on the team that negotiated the merger between SANE and the Freeze Campaign, and then being involved in the early years of Peace Action, is that it was a moment in history when we were part of a national movement that allowed each one of us to be a part of and actually become something far greater than our individual selves. The peace movement of the 1980s, led by SANE and the Freeze, emerged at a time when we felt deeply connected to countless other activists many zip codes and time zones away. Whenever grassroots activists met to plan a trip to Washington, D.C., organize a teach-in, or share in a strategy session, we were aware that people like us were meeting in houses of worship and public school cafeterias all across the country. We developed bonds with activists we had never met, but whom we talked or wrote to, exchanging ideas, offering support, and sharing success stories.

The peace movement and our association first with SANE/Freeze and later Peace Action gave grassroots activists like me a sense of power and connection that made all our work seem valuable and significant. I have tried through the years to convey to my now-18-year-old son what it was like to be part of a peace movement that was so active that each week brought some creative new plan to effect change, a time so filled with possibility that the air seemed to crackle. It is impossible to convey what those years felt like, for we were consumed by peace movement activity and empowered by the influence we had over state and national elected officials, and our staff of activists working together felt like family.

Because I was only a child during the civil rights movement and then active in the anti-Vietnam War movement while a college student, the peace movement of the 1980s provided the first time in my adult life that I was able to devote myself to almost full-time activism and feel the joy, pride, fatigue, delight, and challenge of "movement work." As the director of training for the Peace Development Fund, I traveled nationwide during the 1980s, visiting grassroots peace and justice groups—many of which were affiliated with SANE/Freeze. The diversity and strength of the SANE/Freeze groups from Maine to New Mexico, Oregon to North Carolina, were deeply moving to me as I witnessed grandmothers and teenagers, professional people and working-class folks, clergy and parishioners, professors and their students, all working together on plans to rent buses to take people to a nearby march, evening programs to educate folks about the cost of the Cold War, scenarios for engaging in civil disobedience, and interfaith worship services focusing on peace.

What I witnessed crisscrossing the nation for almost a decade was the vitality and vigor of a movement that had intentionally worked on being multiracial, cross-class, intergenerational, and interfaith. There were struggles as peace group after peace group focused their attention, not just on external political issues, but also on issues of dismantling racism (in their own organizations and in the wider society); sharing power between men and women; and involving working people, not just in large events, but in strategy sessions when projects were chosen and goals were established. As I traveled, I felt a shared commitment in the movement to tackle these difficult issues of racism, classism, sexism, anti-Semitism, and ageism; and those elevated to positions of power reflected the good work done on the grassroots level in confronting these issues. The work was never easy, but the feeling was that our commitment to the peace movement was greater than our individual differences and personal agendas. There was a sense of solidarity that kept us together even when painful issues threatened to divide us.

Although the merger of SANE and the Freeze produced some serious problems—including confusion about the lines of authority and decreased overall funding—the new organization undertook a number of very successful ventures. In 1988, SANE/Freeze joined peace and environmental groups in forming the Plutonium Challenge, which assailed the nuclear weapons complex on health, safety, and environmental grounds. As a result, both the U.S. and Soviet governments began closing their nuclear weapons facilities. Furthermore, SANE/Freeze, along with other peace groups, increasingly focused on securing a Comprehensive

Test Ban Treaty (CTBT). By 1989, the campaign for a test ban was taking off, with the U.S. Comprehensive Test Ban Coalition, headed by Carolyn Cottom, drawing together dozens of peace groups, including SANE/Freeze. Peace activists from around the world converged on Soviet test sites, eventually shutting them down. In the United States, SANE/Freeze pressed forward with the test ban campaign and, in 1992, helped to push legislation through Congress that ended U.S. nuclear testing. During the following years, its successor, Peace Action, kept the pressure on the Clinton administration until, in 1996, the president joined officials from nations around the world in signing a CTBT.[2]

Lessons Learned from the Peace Movement of the 1980s

Although we faced some serious setbacks and disappointments, and sometimes pushed ourselves past the point of physical and mental exhaustion, the peace movement of the 1980s was a high time—a time of many successes, a time of feeling truly connected to a network of wonderful and committed folks from coast to coast. Those years made a permanent imprint on my political views and my engagement with the world. Although now a stodgy, middle-aged mother, I am still an activist who refuses to let go of that part of my identity and my past.

I believe we can glean a number of important lessons from our experiences in the peace movement of the 1980s. What follows are some personal reflections on the lessons learned from the years spent "in the trenches" working with SANE/Freeze and grassroots activists nationwide.

Process Matters!

Although we were always eager to plan the next major event, organize a speak-out with big names, and advertise a workshop on war tax resistance, time spent on *how* the work gets done is as important as doing the actual work itself. The hours and hours we spent making sure that our grassroots groups were welcoming and inclusive was time well spent. The workshops we organized and led on dismantling the "isms" both in the world and in our own peace organizations was time well spent. The careful and sensitive planning that brought SANE and the Freeze Campaign into one larger and more powerful merged organization was time well spent. The way we did our work, with shared power and active and rotating facilitators, all mattered. When working in a social movement, it is important not to fall into the trap of looking, sounding, feeling, and operating like a big corporation even when that is tempting because it is more efficient. Efficiency can eliminate good process, and Monica Green especially led us to learn well that hearing all voices, shared decision-making, and taking the time to be thoughtful and attentive to details and feelings, made for a strong and inclusive movement.

Cover the Waterfront

We learned through our own successes and failures that the best organizing strategies involved many very different entry points for people. The more we offered different ways to be involved in peace movement activities, the more successful we were. For some people, writing a letter or two or three feels like a big step and taking a risk. For some people, standing up in front of their church or synagogue and speaking about their commitment to nonviolence seems appealing and do-able. For some people, direct action or civil disobedience is something they would like to participate in—with the right preparation and training. The more and varied the options were for individuals to get involved, the more people we reached and the more effective our message was.

I remember talking years ago to a woman who thought it was a big step to *attend* a peace march as an observer. She did not want even to consider marching, but thought it would make a statement simply to go and wave from the sidelines. Whatever step people want to take to be involved, even small baby steps, should be honored and valued. The more entry points into a movement, and the more affirmation that every step, every action is significant, the more empowered individuals feel; and that will encourage them to continue taking steps in their own way, in their own time.

Take the Long View

Although movements are full of eager activists who want to see significant, permanent change happen quickly, we must remember that real social change takes decades. If we take the long view, remembering the years that movements from the nineteenth and twentieth centuries struggled until they achieved their goals, we can settle in for the long haul, knowing that we cannot judge our success on one initiative, one ballot question, one town meeting, one election. The real work of social change is only apparent when one reflects on a whole decade of organizing efforts. Cosmetic change comes quickly. Deep and significant change means involving and touching hundreds of thousands of individuals, and that takes time.

Although it is a cliché, the well-known message seen on many bumper stickers is true: "When the people lead, eventually the leaders will follow." People leading and dragging leaders along after years of struggle is exactly what happens in movement work, and it is slow. Leaders or power holders rarely instigate radical social change—it is not in their best interest, and they do not believe the people at home will support them. Movements are made up of those people at home who do unglamorous and often thankless work to change hearts and minds in their own communities. Eventually the leaders come on board when the groundswell below them carries them along.

Taking the long view means expecting setbacks and relaxing about them. Knowing that real change takes decades also allows activists to pace themselves along the journey. If you anticipate running a marathon, you do not push yourself to the limit in the first five miles.

The peace movement of the 1980s was the context in which many of us found and defined our activist selves. The giants of the time in terms of national organizations with money, vision, and clout were SANE and the Nuclear Weapons Freeze Campaign. SANE/Freeze was changed by our experiences, insights, wisdom, and decisions. And in turn it changed our lives as we grew with it and helped it become the powerful and stable organization eventually known as Peace Action.

As I look back on the years I spent "inside" SANE/Freeze, I am filled with gratitude for the energy, spunk, willingness, courage, creativity, and love we showed and shared. Bravo to all of us for touching and changing so many lives and making a chapter in history tilt ever so slightly toward peace and justice.

Notes

1. The previous three paragraphs use information from Monica Green, with thanks.

2. For this paragraph, I owe thanks to Lawrence Wittner; and thanks to Glen Stassen at a few other points.

Chapter 11

Peace Action: 50 Years in the International Peace Movement

Cora Weiss and Ria Pugeda

Peace Action understands that it is part of the international movement for peace. In its own words, Peace Action envisions "a world of peace where war has been abolished as a method of solving conflicts."[1] Its international involvement threads through the histories of its predecessors, SANE and the Nuclear Weapons Freeze Campaign.

In 1958, a year after the founding of SANE, the United Nations accredited SANE to the Department for Public Information as a Non-Governmental Organization (NGO). Donald Keys was SANE's first NGO representative to the UN and was succeeded in turn by Homer Jack, Tudja Crowder, Robert Alpern, David Cortright, Herbert Brandon, and Inge Humbert.[2] In addition, SANE's early leaders maintained good relations with overseas peace groups, especially Britain's Campaign for

Nuclear Disarmament, and in the early 1960s played a key role in the establishment of a new organization that brought them together: the International Confederation for Disarmament and Peace. Recalling this period, Marcus Raskin, a former chair of the SANE board, said: "SANE had a presence at the UN with Norman Cousins' contacts there," but eventually, the UN mostly "dropped off SANE's agenda" and the international peace network dwindled. SANE remained primarily "a domestic organization."[3]

In 1981, the Nuclear Weapons Freeze Campaign designated Glen Stassen as its representative to the European peace movements. He alerted the European movements to the existence and strategy of the Freeze Campaign, since the Freeze was then in its grassroots-building phase and had not yet gone public. On behalf of the Freeze, Stassen persuaded German General Wolf Graf von Baudissin to propose to the German government that it invite the Dutch government to join it in proposing "The Zero Solution," banning all nuclear-tipped medium-range nuclear missiles.[4] It worked: the Germans and Dutch did propose the Zero Solution at the NATO Defense Ministers Conference in Glen-eagles, Scotland. Soviet President Gorbachev accepted the initiative at Reykjavik, and this was a key step in ending the Cold War.

In 1988, a year after the merger, SANE/Freeze formed an International Committee composed of board members. The Committee agreed both to represent the organization at the UN as an NGO and to relate to peace organizations abroad. SANE/Freeze also formally opened its International Office in New York City. Although SANE and the Freeze undertook international work before the merger, this was the first time that a U.S. peace organization created an International Program and opened an International Office.

"Imperialism Is Not Parochial"

Recalling the international work after the merger, Raskin observed that the SANE/Freeze board "had a hard time letting the international dimension into meetings," but "the International Committee attempted to demonstrate that the peace movement could not be parochial because imperialism is not parochial."[5] Raskin maintained that dealing with the United Nations was not enough. There had to be a broader engagement with other peace organizations.

Raskin observed that it was important to the peace movements around the world that they had come to have a sense of continuity and connection through Cora Weiss's work in New York as director of Riverside Church's Disarmament Program, and then to connect with SANE/Freeze when she was appointed SANE/Freeze international representative. He added: "In 1987 SANE/Freeze developed a series of transnational relations with other groups including the International Peace Bureau (IPB) and the Campaign for Nuclear Disarmament." Weiss was elected the first American president of the IPB in 2000 for a six-year term.[6]

Three leaders described the priorities-tension, and the need for an International Office, somewhat differently.

Elizabeth Ainsley Campbell, a former board co-chair, said: "The international arena was always in sight for the mission of SANE/Freeze. But day-to-day organizing occurred within local parameters.... To have an International Office was an important underscoring of our goals."[7]

Steven Brion-Meisels, another former board co-chair, observed: "While we had a sense of global justice, we did not always maintain a focus. The work of Great Neck SANE, Connecticut Peace Action, and Cora reminded us as members that there is a larger world. But it was a struggle for us. Cora reminded us by bringing people from abroad to congresses. It broadened the perspective of folks. It reminded us that there is a world out there."[8]

Bob Moore, director of New Jersey Coalition for Peace Action, said: "Thinking globally and acting locally was more than a slogan. People understood that the issue of peace was a global issue. The possibility of war meant the destruction of the planet in thirty minutes or less. We have to see ourselves as part of an international campaign."

Internationalizing the Hearts and Minds of Peace Activists

The International Office of SANE/Freeze operated out of a donated space at the United Methodist Women's building, which was ideally located across from the UN. Known by its address, 777 UN Plaza, the building was also the home of many peace and justice groups. The International Office shared its space with church programs and representatives from peoples' organizations, including groups from El Salvador and Guatemala, which called on UN members to support human rights and social justice in their countries.

The International Office focused on informing and engaging SANE/ Freeze members on international issues, building and strengthening partnerships with peace organizations throughout the world, and advocating at the United Nations. The first International Committee was composed of Jane Milliken, Colby Lowe, and Pauline Cantwell from Connecticut; and Judy Lerner, Peter Davies, Shirley Romaine, and Cora Weiss from New York, with Ria Pugeda as staffperson of the International Office. According to Weiss, Ria set the tone and standards for the work of the Committee. Later staff included Sister Betty Obal and Tracy Moavero.

SANE/Freeze chapters invited Weiss to speak at meetings and events throughout the country from White Plains, New York, to Hawaii. She spoke for "glasnost," against the Persian Gulf War, and about Euromissiles. In later years, she spoke on women, peace, and security. She organized events to bring together representatives of peace organizations abroad and SANE/Freeze and Peace Action members. In looking back on her years of being a member of the International Committee and serving as the international representative, Weiss said: "We simply did what we thought was natural, honoring Joseph Rotblat, organizing an international conference on small arms, handing out UN umbrellas for good work, hosting Soviets in an anti-Soviet time, providing platforms for Israelis and Palestinians to talk together—whatever. We never thought we were making history, or even making waves."[9]

During the annual conferences an award was given to SANE/Freeze members for their international work. For example, in 1996, Cantwell and Milliken from Connecticut received the International Award.

Engagement in SANE/Freeze's international work expanded to student interns, who were involved in designing and implementing activities. The interns came from universities in the New York City area and included the second generation children of immigrant families.

SANE/Freeze and Peace Action organized conferences and participated in protests on peace and justice issues that connected us with international peace movements. In 1990, before the Persian Gulf War, and in 2003, before the invasion of Iraq, Peace Action joined millions worldwide in protest.

At the SANE/Freeze conference in 1990, a panel on New Politics for a New World was convened with speakers from the Soviet Union, the United States, Hungary, Angola, and a representative of the Palestinian people.

In 1991, SANE/Freeze organized an international conference in New York City, co-sponsored by the Riverside Church Disarmament Program, calling for a halt to the international arms trade. SANE/Freeze volunteers from Connecticut, New York, and New Jersey, and SANE/Freeze members from across the country, were crucial to its success.

The International Committee organized fundraising events with support from celebrities, including a gathering at the Beekman Towers with singer Carly Simon. In 1997, a gathering at Tavern on the Green in New York City honored Admiral Eugene Carroll, Wade Greene from the Rockefeller family philanthropy, and William Sloane Coffin Jr. Present at the event were actress Jane Alexander, singer Judy Collins, and Australian Ambassador Richard Butler, chairman of the Canberra Commission on the Elimination of Nuclear Weapons.

Building Partnerships with International Peace Organizations

Prior to the merger, SANE and Freeze members collaborated on joint projects with international peace groups. For example, in 1985, Jesse Jackson, Justine Merritt, Jane Gruenebaum, David Cortright, and Weiss joined the Women for a Meaningful Summit (WMS) delegation in Geneva, Switzerland. Also present were members of European peace organizations, including Bruce Kent from CND and Petra Kelly and General Gert Bastian from Germany. The visit coincided with the first summit meeting between President Ronald Reagan and U.S.S.R. General Secretary Mikhail Gorbachev. The SANE and Freeze members brought petitions with one million signatures calling for a halt to nuclear testing. On the day of the summit, Sergei Plekanov of the U.S.-Canada Institute arranged for members of the SANE, Freeze, and WMS delegations to meet with Gorbachev. Joe Lelyveld, then a young reporter for the *New York Times,* sensed that a significant event might be emerging and joined the group. The following morning the *New York Times* ran a front page article on Jackson's conversation with Gorbachev. Recalling the exchange, Cortright wrote: "Jackson questioned Gorbachev on the issue of human rights and the plight of Soviet Jews. Gorbachev first tried to avoid the issue. When Jackson pressed him, Gorbachev said that the so-called problem of Soviet Jews doesn't exist."

Despite the Cold War, SANE/Freeze organized exchanges with peace groups in the U.S.S.R. and its allies. We knew that peace groups in the U.S.S.R. lacked the amount of independence from the Soviet government and ability to criticize and prod their government that we enjoyed, and we debated how to relate. We decided that the point was to work for a thaw, and we could contribute to that objective while retaining our realistic awareness that the social locations, freedom, and independence of our two sets of movements were significantly different.

In 1988, the International Office organized a diverse SANE/Freeze delegation to Moscow to experience glasnost under Gorbachev. It included Coffin, Weiss, Campbell from Massachusetts, Cortright from Washington, D.C., Tim Wapato from Oregon, Diana McCook from Tennessee, and Randy Coffin and Jessica Tidman from Vermont. Coffin had a lively conversation with Gorbachev at the Kremlin. Wapato, a Native American, gave an Indian blanket to Raisa Gorbacheva during a reception she hosted for women. The delegation also traveled to Tashkent, met with Russian soldiers AWOL from the Afghan war, and broke bread with Muslim religious leaders.

In 1989, SANE/Freeze hosted a delegation of peace activists from across the former U.S.S.R. The Russian peace activists traveled to different cities and held dialogues with local SANE/Freeze members. These face-to-face interactions were crucial in developing trust between peace activists in the United States and the U.S.S.R. Sylvia Temmer, member of the International Committee and the New Jersey chapter, was hosting Elena Ershova, one of the Russian peace activists, when events leading to the fall of the Berlin Wall were shown on television. She recalled: "All night we sat watching, glued to our sets, waiting for the shots to ring out and the dead to fall. It didn't happen. We were stunned with incredulity."

In 1989, the International Office issued a statement protesting the crackdown on protesters at Tiananmen Square in China. Also in 1989, in response to an invitation from a peace group in East Germany, a SANE/Freeze delegation composed of A.C. Byrd, Karen Jacob, Cortright, and Pugeda visited East Berlin, meeting with representatives of peace groups, churches, environmental organizations, and local communities. No one foresaw the events that occurred a few weeks later, when the Berlin Wall fell.

Sylvia and George Temmer and observers from other countries went to Hungary in 1989 to observe the departure of the Russian troops. She recalled: "When one hears the roar of dozens of military tanks so close

William Sloane Coffin Jr., sings Russian songs in his Washington, D.C., home to entertain Russian visitors, while journalist Seymour Hersh stands in the doorway and Nick Carter, SANE/Freeze executive director, smiles in the foreground, ca. 1990 (Cora Weiss).

that you can touch them as they roll by, one cannot help but wonder at the awe and fear they invoked as they roared into Hungary years before. Yet, here they were rolling out of their garages onto railroad sidings and leaving Hungary. Also, surprisingly here were those young Russian conscripts who accepted our peace buttons, pinned them on their uniforms and paraded down the streets to the troop trains in military formation wearing those buttons." Later a retired Russian general, a peace activist, held a piece of the barbed wire which separated Hungary and Austria, while Sylvia cut the wire in pieces.

Temmer also helped mobilize a delegation of 16 people to the 1999 Hague Appeal for Peace conference in the Netherlands. It was a strong delegation, with five members from high schools around the country who were selected through a national essay contest. Brion-Meisels considered the Hague Appeal for Peace conference "a quantum leap for SANE/Freeze. In May 1999, young people, members of chapters, folks from the national structure all went to The Hague and met like-minded people from around the world."

The Hague conference was organized by the Hague Appeal for Peace; Cora Weiss, then a board member of Peace Action and a leader of our

Cora Weiss embraces actor and peace activist Ossie Davis at a Peace Action event, held at the Ethical Culture Society in New York City, celebrating the 20th anniversary of the massive June 12, 1982, antinuclear demonstration, June 2002 *(Cora Weiss)*.

International Committee, was and is president of the Hague Appeal, and deserves credit for much of the vision and the organizing (editor's comment). Peace Action members were among the 10,000 people participating. It was the largest peace conference in history, according to ABC news.

Individual members also represented SANE/Freeze at various international meetings and events. In 1996, Jane Milliken attended the UN's Habitat II Conference in Turkey. She was in Nicaragua in 1990 to observe the national elections, along with Coffin and Weiss. Bob Moore visited Scandinavia and Greece, where he met peace movement leaders from around the world. "My trip to Scandinavia," he later remarked, "resulted in our chapter offering home stays to 70 members of the Nordic Women for Peace who walked from New York to Washington. They passed through Princeton and later offered us reciprocity."

SANE/Freeze officially joined the International Peace Bureau, the world body of peace organizations, in 1991. Colin Archer, IPB's secretary, recalled: "It was the year the U.S.S.R. was broken up and a time when the hopes for the 'peace dividend' following the end of the Cold War were perhaps at their highest." He added: "Peace Action has been a loyal supporter of and cooperator with IPB in international actions ranging from anti-nuclear efforts (Test Ban Campaign, World Court Project, Non-Proliferation Treaty, and Abolition 2000) to work on the arms trade and military spending."

United Nations: Thinking Locally, Acting Globally

SANE/Freeze and Peace Action's accreditation as an NGO at the United Nations has been essential for its international work. In 1987, the Board approved a resolution to "establish a relationship with the UN that includes non-governmental status—the primary aim of which is to participate and keep abreast of the international community's work in the field of disarmament and other issues we deem appropriate to our interest." Following Weiss, the second NGO representative was the late Irving Lerner, co-chairperson of Westchester, NY, Nuclear Weapons Freeze Campaign. Lerner wrote:

> My 15 months at the NGO world of the UN has taught me about its programs, its achievements and failures, but mostly it has internationalized my peace consciousness. I have become more aware of the Third World, its needs, problems, and possible solutions. I believe that it is essential for all of us, particularly those in the peace movement, to educate ourselves about this impressively housed establishment. If we are to think globally and act locally we need the UN. But we must also think locally and act globally.[10]

The NGO representatives and SANE/Freeze members worked with the UN's NGO Committee on Disarmament, met with representatives of the UN, and reported on meetings that addressed conventional and nuclear disarmament, reduction of military budgets, and confidence-building measures. In 1988, after the collapse of the Third UN Special Session on Disarmament, Lerner wrote: "The non-aligned and developing countries will not soon forget or forgive the intransigent and self-serving role the U.S. played in the failure of SSOD III."[11] Despite the setback, Lerner found "a glimmer of hope" in the presence of more than 900 NGOs representing peace and church groups, labor unions, and environmental groups, "which have the potential of becoming a worldwide peace network."

Judy Lerner succeeded Irving and presently serves as the third NGO representative at the United Nations. She also heads the International

Committee, which has some 20 members from the Greater New York area. In 2001, Judy wrote that our effort in the past, as it is now, has been to encourage greater grassroots participation and understanding of the importance of the peacemaking activity of the United Nations and to integrate it wherever possible in our local work. The International Committee provides a venue for speakers on the Comprehensive Test Ban Treaty, sanctions, and ending bloodshed in Africa and the Middle East, as well as arms trafficking.[12] Acknowledging the volunteerism and commitment of Peace Action members, Judy wrote: "None of this could or would happen were it not for a dedicated few who spend days and sometimes nights at the United Nations." Judy herself has traveled for Peace Action to Rhodesia, Afghanistan, South Africa, Israel, and Palestine.

During its early years, the International Office organized tours of the UN for SANE/Freeze members, and "Tea Time for Talk"—a series of forums on global security where members of the UN were invited to speak and engage in conversation with SANE/Freeze members.

SANE/Freeze and Peace Action members actively participated in UN conferences on disarmament, small arms, culture of peace, racism, and children in armed conflict. Members played important roles during the annual UN Department of Public Information/NGO conferences. On September 10, 2001, Peace Action co-sponsored a workshop entitled "A Dialogue on Best Practices for Volunteer Peace Workers." The participants were so engaged in the discussion that they decided to re-convene the next day. However, the attacks on the World Trade Center on September 11 changed the course of events—for us as well as for U.S. policy.

Commitment to a New U.S. Foreign Policy: Real Security through International Cooperation and Human Rights

As Cortright has noted, over the years Peace Action has undergone a radical change as it has developed a "synergy between civil society and diplomats." The American peace movement had a "significant impact on the build-up to the Iraq war, joining with world public opinion in massive rallies in February 2003 that led to influencing the Security Council to refuse to fall in with the U.S." government.

In 2003, Peace Action launched a major campaign "to promote a new U.S. foreign policy based on peaceful support for human rights and democracy, reducing the threat from weapons of mass destruction, and cooperation with the world community."[13] This emphasis on moving beyond nationalism has long characterized Peace Action. As Coffin said in a television message in 1991: "The world would be a safer and saner place if somehow we Americans got over our self-righteousness in our foreign relations."[14] Thus, today, Peace Action renews its commitment as part of the international peace movement to engage its grassroots members and U.S. policymakers in achieving real security through international cooperation and human rights.

Notes

1. Peace Action Web site, www.peace-action.org.

2. United Nations, Department of Public Information, New York City, New York.

3. Interview with Marcus Raskin by Cora Weiss, September 14, 2006.

4. Glen Stassen, *Just Peacemaking: Transforming Initiatives for Justice and Peace* (Louisville: Westminster John Knox, 1992), 116-34.

5. Raskin.

6. Written comments of Marcus Raskin, September 21, 2006.

7. Interview with Elizabeth Ainsley Campbell by Cora Weiss, September 15, 2006.

8. Interview with Steven Brion-Meisels by Cora Weiss, September 14. 2006.

9. Written comments of Cora Weiss, September 19, 2006.

10. Personal document of Irving Lerner entitled "The Education of an NGO."

11. Irving Lerner, "U.S. Criticized for Failure of Third Special Session on Disarmament," SANE/Freeze of Westchester Newsletter, October 1988.

12. Judy Lerner, Peace Action International Committee report, February 2001.

13. Peace Action Web site, www.peace-action.org.

14. Message by William Sloane Coffin Jr., "Not to Bring Peace, But a Sword," Program #3519, first broadcast February 16, 1992, *30 Good Minutes.*

The Strength of Peace Action's Affiliate Network: A View from the Left Coast

Jon Rainwater

Former House Speaker Tip O'Neill used to say "All politics is local," to communicate the power local views and interests can have on national decisions. In an era when the United States plays the "world's sole superpower" role, the expression takes on *increased* meaning. "All politics is local" still applies, even when those politics are about a war raging halfway around the globe.

Peace Action's affiliate network is the embodiment of that political truth. Peace Action has nearly 100 state or regional affiliates and chapters. There is great variety in the tactics these affiliates employ, but affiliates all make the politics of Peace Action a local politics. In chilly New England winters, New Hampshire Peace Action combines the local with the national by raising the profile of Peace Action's issues during that state's early presidential primary. In the high desert of the Southwest, Peace Action New Mexico keeps a watchful eye on the nuclear weapons work at Los Alamos and Sandia national laboratories.

This chapter focuses on the practice of local politics from the viewpoint of the largest of the network's affiliates: Peace Action West. Previously California Peace Action, Peace Action West was founded in 2006. As Peace Action celebrates 50 years of waging peace, California Peace Action is being reborn as Peace Action West to recognize our organization's burgeoning role in the western states. Our region's geographic size and diversity has caused us to develop a unique blend of local organizing tactics. But for Peace Action West, one type of grassroots organizing stands out: Peace Action West is the house that field canvassing built. We've built a large membership in liberal bastions like the Bay Area and Los Angeles. But we've also built grassroots capacity in more far-flung areas and more conservative areas. We now have close to 50,000 supporters. Canvassing has also served as an introduction to grassroots organizing for thousands of young activists. Peace Action canvassing alumni are sprinkled throughout the peace and justice movement.

As we've grown the ranks of our members, we've been driven by the desire to have our preaching reach beyond the choir. The person whose door we are knocking on is more often a suburban soccer mom or dad thinking about getting their kids to bed than a Berkeley or Hollywood activist worrying about the latest incursion of the American empire. Through this outreach, busy people without a strong activist identity are provided a vehicle for participating in critical U.S. foreign policy debates.

We've also "power mapped" our membership recruitment by targeting the most politically significant or swing districts. We've grown grassroots clout in many of the congressional districts of members of the House Armed Services and International Relations committees. Also, as we organize in each district we choose a clear political mission. Often this means gathering hundreds or thousands of hand-written constituent letters for targeted "swing votes" in Congress. A recent study by the Congressional Management Foundation showed that personalized letters are by far the most persuasive form of individual constituent communication. Ninety-six percent of Congressional staff members said that the letters would have influence in their boss's decision-making process. (Forty-four percent said "a lot of influence" and 52 percent said "some influence."[1])

One historical anecdote illustrates the power of simple grassroots action by "regular folks" to shape history. It tells the story of how former speaker Tip O'Neill learned that all politics is local. In 1966, O'Neill was a staunch supporter of the Vietnam War who thought the war's opponents were "kooks, commies and egghead professors." But in 1966, something got his attention. As a leading biographer of O'Neill has noted: "He could dismiss the generic postcards that arrived by the dozen by earnest leftist groups with names like 'Individuals Against the Crime of Silence.' But the handwritten letters from the working families of North Cambridge, Brighton, and Somerville commanded his attention, and, sitting at his desk in his stocking feet, fiddling with his rosary beads or small change in his pocket, he struggled to send more than a form letter in reply."[2] This local kind of pressure led to a change of heart for O'Neill, who became perhaps the most important congressional leader in the movement to bring the troops home.

Learning to Listen:
The Message and Media Environment

These core organizing strategies have provided us with an important lesson: they have taught us to listen. We've learned that it's not enough to get out raw facts about policy or simply "to speak truth to (or about) power." Our staff has learned how to listen to feedback at the door and to "cut the issues" to different audiences. We've had to craft messages for an audience that is diverse ethnically, geographically, and class-wise.

In the media, at the door, and with potential alliance partners we've also had to fight against a stereotype of the peace movement as a constituency that is outside of the political mainstream. The right wing has a patented blend of ridicule mixed with a dollop of fear that has successfully undermined many a progressive cause. Visceral culturally based stereotypes portray progressive concerns as elitist or "fringe." Environmentalists (picture them wearing Birkenstocks) are "tree huggers" out to take your jobs. Labor "bosses" (picture them smoking a cigar) are "greedy."

The peace movement has a particularly tough hill to climb when it comes to these stereotypes. In this era, many politicians fear the charge "soft on defense" more than any other epithet. The way the communications media cover our issues also marginalizes peace and justice advocacy groups. When covering environmental issues or issues of reproductive choice, it would be natural to feature a spokesperson from Sierra Club or NARAL. But on issues of war and peace, the media turn to military experts, diplomats or—on a good day—a sympathetic voice from a think tank. Peace and justice groups need to be creative to position themselves as legitimate spokespeople.

Because of this uphill fight, our organization has taken to heart all the recent attention on "framing" and "values-based" language. Peace Action West produces internal message guidance and talking points for each of our priority campaigns, and we ground our message in values-based, everyday language.

Part of our strategy for getting our message into the mainstream media has been to pay to put out our messages unedited. We've done this in full-page newspaper advertisements, radio and cable TV ads, and through billboards and posters in transit systems.

Although we've worked to craft messages based on mainstream values and principles, that doesn't mean that we have shied away from hard-hitting messages or biting satire. For example, one of our ads undermined the administration's position during the early days of the Iraq war by pointing out that the United States had offered military support to Saddam Hussein. The ad featured a picture of Donald Rumsfeld, then a Reagan administration envoy, shaking Saddam Hussein's hand with a headline that asked: "Who Are We Arming Now?" The image was hard hitting, but the language was grounded in Americans' desire for policies that are principled and consistent. Our "We've Found the Weapons of Mass Destruction" ads highlighted President Bush's planned development of a new generation of nuclear weapons. This campaign was part of the successful effort to cut funds for development of low-yield nuclear weapons and nuclear bunker-busters. These ads described the administration's nuclear stance as a "do as we say not as we do" policy that failed the test of common sense and pragmatism.

We've even had a fair amount of success in getting out our message on talk radio—a media environment usually associated with conservative points of view. Our reliance on mainstream-friendly messaging has found surprisingly strong support from moderate and even conservative talk show hosts.

Broadening the Base, Broadening Ourselves

Our movement must also do a better job of articulating what a foreign policy based on our values looks like. As George Lakoff, the leading progressive evangelist of "framing," wrote shortly before the start of the Iraq war:

> First the anti-war movement properly understood is not just, or even primarily, a movement against the war. It is a movement against the overall direction the Bush administration is moving in.
> Second, to be effective such a movement needs to be able to say what it is for, not just what it is against.
> Third it must have a clearly articulated moral vision, with values rather than mere interests determining its political direction.[3]

After September 11, 2001, we felt even stronger about the imperative to reach out to the broadest constituency possible. The political landscape for foreign policy issues underwent one of its periodic tectonic shifts, and for a time dissent on foreign policy issues was hard to come by. But we also sensed a desire at the grassroots for a unified opposition to the Bush administration's unilateral approach to foreign policy. That desire was quite diffuse and it was more a critique than a vision. The Bush administration had a clear vision for the world and we needed one, too.

Peace Action West worked with the Peace Action affiliate network to create the Campaign for a New Foreign Policy. We called for a foreign policy rooted in international cooperation and we opposed the Bush doctrine of preemption. In many ways this campaign was a precursor to Peace Action's "Real Security through International Cooperation and Human Rights" platform described elsewhere in this volume.

We shared this campaign with the faith community, with women's groups, and with organizations representing communities of color as we made presentations in community halls and local congregations. Even at a time when the wounds of September 11 were still raw, this campaign received strong support. From 2002 to 2004 we signed up over 100 organizations and key individuals, representing well over a million Americans, to the campaign. We received endorsements from county labor councils and from dozens of members of the state assembly and city council members, as well as from many Democratic clubs and Democratic Party committees.

At the same time as we have worked to broaden the constituencies we work with, we have worked to create an organization that reflects the diversity of our region. We have put in place a number of programs to diversify board, staff, and membership. We have a long-term diversity plan, we've developed a political activist apprenticeship program for organizers of color, and we hold trainings and dialogues to foster a multicultural workplace. We are working to embody the diversity we wish to see throughout the peace movement.

Changing the Playing Field

In one of SANE's first forays into electoral politics, SANE joined with other activists in supporting more than twenty peace candidates in races during the mid-term election of 1962.[4] Since then, SANE, the Freeze, and Peace Action have approached electoral politics using two separate but complementary approaches. At times we have taken sides in critical races through tactics like endorsements, field organizing, electoral paid and earned media, and financial and in-kind contributions. At other times we have employed voter education techniques that do not support one candidate over another but instead raise the profile of our issues through tactics like candidate briefings and non-partisan voter guides.

The importance and impact of electoral strategies to elect "peace candidates" directly has waxed and waned during the 50 years of Peace Action history. Elsewhere in this volume, Lawrence Wittner points out that SANE was the "first non-partisan group to oppose the reelection of Lyndon Johnson and the first to support the peace candidacy of Eugene McCarthy." Freeze Voter was founded in 1984 to "elect a President and Congress who will enact a nuclear weapons Freeze between the U.S. and the U.S.S.R." A writer for *Mother Jones* pointed out that Freeze Voter "represented a significant departure from the peace movement's traditional avoidance of electoral politics." Involved in over 40 races, Freeze Voter mobilized 20,000 volunteers and raised nearly $3.5 million for extensive grassroots electoral campaigns.[5]

The unpopular war in Iraq has encouraged us to return to electing "peace candidates" forty-four years after SANE piloted that strategy. Peace Action West joined with partners in the Peace Action network to support about two dozen candidates through contributions, endorsements, and grassroots organizers. We placed organizers in key districts with close races in California, Washington, New Mexico, and Arizona. At the same time we ran Get Out The Vote (GOTV) phone banks to reach voters in those states as well as in Colorado. Working directly to elect the candidates who agree with our positions allows us to change the political playing field in a way that can vastly increase the chances of moving our agenda.

The 2006 elections can be interpreted as a mandate for change in the country's Iraq policy and more broadly as a mandate for a more peaceful, more cooperative foreign policy. But we need to build upon that victory if we want a strong and permanent voting bloc for peace. Peace Action West believes the peace movement needs to maintain a robust electoral program similar to what Freeze Voter had in 1984 if we want to fundamentally change the direction of foreign policy in this country.

Coordinated Campaigns and Grassroots Capacity: A Tale of Two Treaties

The arc of the Cold War and its aftermath delineates some of Peace Action's biggest victories and defeats. Near the beginning of the Cold War, SANE played a critical role in securing the first nuclear arms control treaty—the Partial Test Ban Treaty. As the Cold War entered its final chapter, both SANE and the Freeze fostered a groundswell that forced Congress and even President Reagan to take nuclear arms control and disarmament seriously. Unfortunately, the end of the Cold War era did not usher in the type of peace dividend—economic or metaphorical—that many had hoped it would. The defeat of the Comprehensive Test Ban Treaty in the Senate in 1999 underscored the difficulty of mobilizing grassroots pressure on nuclear issues in a post–Cold War era when the "Soviet threat" had dematerialized.

Locally targeted grassroots power played a crucial role in the passage of the Partial Test Ban Treaty. Political insiders including the White House "saw support from the grassroots as key" and urged "long streams of delegations to senators." A grassroots effort led by SANE launched a "carefully coordinated" campaign that featured ads in local papers, radio outreach to hundreds of local stations, and alliances with the business, faith, labor, and scientific communities. President Kennedy himself personally urged grassroots forces to "get the letters moving" to counter congressional testimony from military forces.[6]

At the dawn of the era of nuclear arms control, this campaign tapped into growing public awareness of the nuclear threat and channeled that awareness into a targeted, multifaceted, grassroots campaign to push the Senate to vote the right way on this signal issue. The results were impressive: in September of 1963, the Senate voted to ratify the treaty 80 to 19.

But at the end of the Cold War, nuclear issues faded from the forefront of people's minds. Jonathan Schell argues that the end of the Cold War took away the conceptual framework—military, political and moral—that allowed the public to perceive the threat of nuclear destruction. That loss could be measured in a decrease in Peace Action membership and dwindling grassroots activity and grassroots capacity.

The defeat of Senate ratification of the Comprehensive Test Ban Treaty (CTBT) was perhaps the clearest embodiment of the weakened political power of our movement in the 1990s. The failure of ratification has been traced to a number of factors that range from a polarized political environment in Washington to opposition from the nuclear weapons labs. But diminished grassroots capacity and a less than ample "outside the beltway" campaign must be part of the story. When the vote came, ratification failed 48 to 51—a resounding loss, given that two-thirds approval was required.

Importantly, the defeat of the CTBT on the Senate floor can be seen as a victory for local grassroots power—it just wasn't *our* grassroots power. When it became clear the treaty would go down in defeat, 24 Senate Republicans joined 38 Democrats and signed a letter asking for the vote to be postponed. But Senate Majority Leader Trent Lott (R-Miss.) ignored his colleagues and brought the treaty to a vote to please "the grassroots activists who provide most of the party's funding and organizational strength." As one top Republican aide said: "The issue had been elevated to the level where it was seen as such a bad treaty, that it would have been very hard to shift gears with our conservative base and not vote on it. They wanted us in the end zone, spiking the ball on something that belonged to Bill Clinton."[7]

The two forces we will need to move the nuclear disarmament agenda are active public concern and carefully coordinated and truly nationwide grassroots efforts. Americans remain very concerned about nuclear weapons. In an Associated Press poll released in March of 2005, a majority of Americans (53%) said they believed that a terrorist attack using nuclear weapons is likely in the following five years, and a similar majority (52%) believe it is likely that one country will attack another country with nuclear weapons in the same time period. We need to galvanize this concern and at the same time significantly improve our capacity to mount a truly national campaign. To do that we need to build a larger, more geographically dispersed grassroots constituency that can be mobilized to get federal policymakers to make the right decisions.

As Martin Luther King Jr. often said in his speeches: "The arc of the moral universe is long, but it bends towards justice." It is the local action of groups like the Peace Action affiliates that creates the pull to bend history's arc: One dramatic advertisement, one swing member of Congress, one alliance partner, one election, and one door, at a time.

Notes

1. Congressional Management Foundation, *Communicating With Congress* (Washington D.C.: Congressional Management Foundation, 2005), 34. Report available at http://www.cmfweb.org/cwcreport1.asp.

2. John A. Farrell, *Tip O'Neill and the Democratic Century* (Boston: Little Brown and Company, 2001), 214–217.

3. George Lakoff, *Don't Think of an Elephant!* (White River Junction, VT: Chelsea Green, 2004), 74.

4. Lawrence S. Wittner, *Resisting the Bomb: A History of the World Nuclear Disarmament Movement, 1954–1970* (Stanford, CA: Stanford University Press, 1997), 263.

5. Records of Freeze Voter, Document Group 156, Swarthmore College Peace Collection. Available online at http://www.swarthmore.edu/Library/peace/.

6. Wittner, *Resisting the Bomb,* 426–427.

7. Terry Deibel, "The Death of a Treaty," *Foreign Affairs* 81 (September/October 2002): 156.

Chapter 13

Peace Action Today

Kevin Martin

In August 2006, at a concert in Saratoga Springs, New York, I was stunned to hear David Crosby, Stephen Stills, Graham Nash and Neil Young sing *a cappella*:

> Who are the men, who really run this land?
> What are their names, and on what streets do they live?
> I'd like to go over this afternoon, and give them a piece of my mind
> About peace for mankind
> Peace is not a lot to ask.

Peace activists everywhere work so hard for the least little bit of progress, and it seems so elusive, but really, peace is not a lot to ask. It is what everyone, everywhere should expect and aspire to—peace in their lives, peace in their communities, peace in the world. It should be the norm, and we should be more assumptive and confident about this in our activism.

Instead our government promises us a seemingly endless "war on terror," and it advocates, threatens, and wages illegal "pre-emptive" wars of aggression while threatening our civil liberties at home. And now other governments are predictably following our lead. To name just a few, Israel, Russia, and even Japan cite the "war on terror" and/or the "right" of "pre-emptive war" to justify their policies.

Peace is not a lot to ask, but we, the people, must demand it, and we must build it. Our government, whether run by Republicans or Democrats, will not just give it to us.

Reflections on Our Mission

I started my career in SANE at the absolute entry level, as a door-to-door canvasser in Washington, D.C., in July 1985 (and also canvassed in Massachusetts and Pennsylvania). Regardless of my personal situation, I think it is cool to have someone who started on the bottom rung of the organization serve years later as executive director.

After working for four years in the canvass operation, where I really cut my teeth as an organizer with some amazing co-workers who remain close friends to this day (and met my wife and companion, Sue Udry), I spent ten wonderful years as executive director of Illinois Peace Action in Chicago from 1989 to 1999. For two years, I directed Project Abolition, a national coalition of groups working for nuclear disarmament, before accepting the job as Peace Action and Peace Action Education Fund's executive director on September 4, 2001, just a week before the horrific attacks of September 11.

I always feel honored and humbled to serve as executive director, but even more so in our organization's 50th anniversary year. I'm only 44 years old, but I've been involved in various roles with the organization for over 22 years now. That's not as long as our development director, Peter Deccy (25 years on staff!), and not as long as many of our volunteer leaders and members, as well as many of my co-authors of this volume. Peace Action has such a loyal membership base, without which we would never have had the opportunity to celebrate our 50th birthday!

Over the last 22 years, I have been blessed to play a small part in many successful campaigns, most of which are noted in this book: stopping military aid to the contras in Nicaragua, cutting off arms sales to

Peace Action staff members and managers, December 2006. Top row (left to right): Graham Cowger (development associate, membership), Paul Kawika Martin (organizing and political director), Eric Swanson (database manager), Kevin Martin (executive director), Gordon Clark (communications director). Middle row (left to right): Yeabu Conteh (development associate), Megan O'Brien (development associate), Katherine Fuchs (organizing and policy associate). Front row (left to right): Ashley Houghton (communications associate), Peter Deccy (development director), Randy Wilson (Student Peace Action organizer), Christina Ulis (membership data coordinator), Rosalie Brooks (director of finance and administration) *(photo by Susan Udry)*.

Indonesia because of its occupation of East Timor, securing the Ottawa Treaty banning anti-personnel landmines (albeit without the U.S. government signing on), obtaining a Comprehensive Test Ban Treaty (albeit still unratified by the Senate), cutting off funding for the Robust Nuclear Earth Penetrator (aka the nuclear bunker buster), as well as helping to take down a few hawkish members of Congress and to replace them with pro-peace legislators.

You will note that many of those victories, like others in our movement's history, were partial, incomplete, or otherwise somewhat compromised. That is often the way, and while we should never lower our sights from the peaceful and just world we know we must achieve, neither should we downplay the successes we have helped deliver.

I see Peace Action's work, while certainly practical and political, as at its core prophetic. In a book of essays by the great author, environmentalist, and advocate of civil disobedience Henry David Thoreau, editor Lewis Hyde describes Thoreau's work as prophetic—not necessarily predictive of future events or conditions, but rather providing a philosophy of living in balance and harmony with nature that is timeless and universal. Similarly, Peace Action's work for peace helps give voice to humanity's quest for peace that transcends eras and, as the whole world should see so clearly now in this time of grave threats, is the only possible way forward for our common future.

Whether we see our work as prophetic, practical, political, or transformational—and we take both our first name (Peace) and our last name (Action) very seriously—the stakes could not possibly be higher. Unless we as a society and as a human family urgently move toward peace, disarmament, social and economic justice, and environmental restoration, the future is indeed bleak. I fear for my children's future and wonder if I will ever have grandchildren, and worry that if I do, they may well inherit a dystopian world of war, fear, greed, and environmental devastation. If we want our species and the planet to survive, we have no choice other than to take personal responsibility (something conservatives advocate) to make the necessary changes.

My observation is that not many in our society understand that yet. As I write this, in the fall of 2006, George W. Bush and his policies are deeply unpopular. Yet I do not see many people willing to make a serious commitment to doing whatever is necessary (non-violently of course) to change government policy, let alone change their own way of life to help ensure a more sustainable lifestyle for our society and the planet. Our job as activists is not to scold—for that is completely ineffective—but rather to shine a light on different possibilities that offer practical solutions to seemingly enormous, intractable problems (which of course are of our society's own making), and to inspire people to take personal responsibility, to act.

We in the peace movement are good at analyzing what is wrong in the world—in fact we are prone to going on at tedious length in this regard. We can also articulate positive alternatives, though we need to strengthen this in order to be more proactive. But have we really come to terms with what will be required of us, what sacrifices we will need to make, in order to achieve our goals?

I don't claim to have the answers to this question; that would be fatuous of me. Instead, my hope is that we, as individuals, as an organization, and as a movement that aspires to transform our society to be truly just and peaceful, will challenge ourselves and turn more of our energies in this direction.

Our Last Name Is Action!

Although our work has always been critically important, the last six years have arguably been the most difficult in Peace Action's half-century history, given the all-out assault on world peace unleashed by the Bush Administration and the political climate of fear it has successfully created and exploited since September 11, 2001. Still, I am amazed and proud every day at the resilience of Peace Action's dedicated grassroots activist and membership base, particularly our affiliates and chapters around the country. In 2003 and 2004, Peace Action's organizing framework was the Campaign for a New Foreign Policy, which promoted a new direction for the United States based on American values of international cooperation and diplomacy, human rights, and a serious commitment to ridding the planet of weapons of mass destruction. California Peace Action conceived the campaign and its staff provided steady leadership for the effort. Over 450 labor, religious, women's, civil rights, community, and peace organizations, as well as local and federal elected officials, endorsed the campaign, which offered a stark contrast to Bush's policies, particularly the disastrous war and occupation of Iraq. The campaign's framework was adapted in 2005 for Peace Action's Long-Range Strategic Plan, Real Security through International Cooperation and Human Rights. It continues to provide an overarching message for our work that connects with the desire of a majority of Americans who want a new direction for U.S. foreign policy.

Peace Voter

Inaugurated in 1996, our one-of-its-kind-in-the-peace-movement Peace Voter campaign has reached tens of millions of voters with non-partisan voter guides comparing and contrasting presidential and congressional candidates' positions on peace and social justice issues. In addition to the voter guides and an informative Web site at peacevoter.org with varied resources and materials for election-related work, Peace Action's Peace Voter activists bird-dog candidates at public appearances, register and help turn out thousands of voters, and—through local media—carry our message that peace is a winning issue in elections. In the 2006 mid-term elections, Peace Action affiliates waged Peace Voter campaigns in over 50 House and Senate races, including some of the most crucial races, in Connecticut, New Hampshire, Pennsylvania, Maryland, New York, New Jersey, Ohio,

Michigan, New Mexico, California, Washington, and other states. Peace Action's political committee, Peace Action PAC, was also active in endorsing or financially supporting candidates in over two dozen races. Since no other peace group wages this kind of non-partisan issue advocacy campaign, Peace Voter 2006 gave concrete form to the peace movement's general success in raising peace and disarmament issues, particularly opposition to the disastrous occupation of Iraq, to the top of the election-year debate agenda.

Peace Voter 2008 promises to be our largest effort to date. In addition to House and Senate races, both the Republican and Democratic presidential nominations will be open with no incumbent, offering a tremendous opportunity to affect the primaries and the national debate on peace issues in what, we hope, will be a "turning point" election for the country.

Presidential candidate bird-dogging in the small but influential state of New Hampshire, with its unique "nobody votes for a candidate they haven't met five times" retail politics, has been very effectively carried out in recent presidential elections by New Hampshire Peace Action (NHPA) and its allies in the state. For the 2008 election cycle, NHPA began training activists and bird-dogging candidates in 2006, as potential candidates are nearly constantly trekking to the Granite State. We hope to help NHPA ramp up its efforts by organizing financial and activist support from outside New Hampshire, and also to replicate its model in Nevada and other early primary states. In the 2004 election, NHPA bird-doggers reported hearing presidential candidates "reflecting our message back at us." And this was no accident; it was the result of training, organizing, and having a clear, simple message on the need for a new foreign policy that activists carried to the candidates and to the public.

We expect the same to be true in the 2008 election, as the public hungers for a new path for our country. Peace Action's Peace Voter 2008 work will likely be one of the most important campaigns to influence the electoral debate on peace and disarmament issues, and to help empower Americans to demand a new foreign policy emphasizing real security through international cooperation and human rights.

Nuclear "Bunker Buster"

Peace Action's steadfast commitment to ridding the world of the scourge of nuclear weapons has manifested itself in many different ways over the last 50 years, as the threats posed by nuclear technology have evolved.

Although we maintain that total global abolition of nuclear weapons is the only solution, we face the necessity of defeating the ever-changing schemes of the Dr. Strangeloves in the nuclear priesthood.

Their latest mad proposal is the Robust Nuclear Earth Penetrator, or "nuclear bunker buster," intended to be a new, more "useable" nuclear weapon—one able to penetrate and destroy hardened targets, such as concrete bunkers sheltering nuclear facilities of "rogue" regimes. It would be used "pre-emptively," before any other nation had initiated nuclear war, thus leaping across the firebreak to nuclear catastrophe.

On its face, seeking to develop a new, more useable nuke while selectively preaching non-proliferation to certain countries is absurd, and most people, even politicians, understand this. (John Kerry made his opposition to the bunker buster, in the same clear, commonsense terms we use, a key issue in his 2004 presidential campaign). "Do as we say, not as we do" seldom works in life, and certainly not in foreign policy.

Such a policy that runs so counter to commonsense cannot long survive. Moreover, independent physicists maintain the weapon would not be able to penetrate hardened targets as advertised, and that exploding the weapon in an urban setting would cause massive casualties. Physicians for Social Responsibility issued a study asserting that an RNEP attack against a potential target, an Iranian nuclear facility in a populated area, would kill 10,000 people and send a radioactive cloud east toward Afghanistan, where thousands of US troops are stationed. From 2002 to 2005, the entire disarmament and arms control community made stopping the RNEP program its top priority for nuclear weapons-related work, gaining some partial successes in cuts to the program before achieving victory by deleting all funding for it in 2004 and 2005. Peace Action helped lead grassroots public education and legislative pressure campaigns against the RNEP. Affiliates and chapters around the country mobilized constituent pressure on key legislators. Peace Action New Mexico and California Peace Action played particularly important roles, including work on a joint public education and media campaign with colleague organizations in New Mexico. In the summer of 2005, we targeted a key backer of the RNEP, Senator Pete Domenici, who thereafter retreated from his personal support of the program.

As organizers, we take seriously the need to strategize—to set concrete objectives, pick the right political targets, and devise appropriate strategies and tactics to achieve our aims—and to evaluate our efforts. What was apparently the most decisive factor in defeating the RNEP was the staunch opposition to it of U.S. Rep. David Hobson of Ohio, a conservative Republican subcommittee chair and normally no friend to the peace movement. But behind this break in Republican ranks was our general success at framing the issue on our terms, making commonsense, jargon-free arguments, and having them gain traction and take hold in the public debate at large and with decision-makers, certainly including Rep. Hobson and other Republican lawmakers who otherwise support almost all of Bush's national security priorities.

However, the Dr. Strangeloves never quit. As Ronald Reagan might say: "There they go again!" Late last year, the Department of Energy announced a $155 billion program to re-build the U.S. nuclear weapons production complex to near Cold War capacity by the year 2030. Dubbed "Complex 2030" by its supporters, this plan has been quickly re-dubbed "Bombplex 2030" by enterprising peace activists. Although the peace and disarmament movement will need to mobilize public and congressional opposition in order to stop this lunacy, it also provides us with the opportunity to demand that the U.S. government commit itself to the global abolition of nuclear weapons and, in the meantime, to a responsible, non-hypocritical, non-proliferation policy.

Iraq

In the spring and summer of 2002, I was very concerned that Peace Action and the rest of the peace movement were not sufficiently alarmed at the Bush administration's clear intention to invade Iraq. However, in the fall, we made up for lost time. In just a few months, large national coalitions including ANSWER (Act Now to Stop War and End Racism), United for Peace and Justice (UFPJ), and Win Without War—with Peace Action a founding member of the latter two coalitions—came together, along with the National Youth and Student Peace Coalition (formed in response to the war with Afghanistan), to mobilize millions of Americans to oppose war with Iraq before it began.

Peace Action led the first large demonstration in Washington against a potential war with Iraq in September 2002. A high-spirited crowd of over 5,000 marched along Embassy Row to cheers from many embassy personnel (South Africa's in particular), ending at Vice President Dick Cheney's residence. The march was much smaller than similar anti-war rallies in Europe that weekend but still garnered significant local, national, and international media coverage.

Peace Action helped mobilize for much larger demonstrations in the coming months, especially UFPJ's huge "The World Says No to War" rally in Manhattan on February 15, 2003. That day, in the largest political demonstration in human history, over 12 million people around the world protested against a U.S. war on Iraq, prompting *The New York Times* to call the peace movement the world's second superpower.

Unfortunately, nothing could deter the Bush administration from launching the war. (President Bush himself, in one of the more out-of-touch moments of a detached presidency, dismissed the huge demonstrations as "a focus group.") A predictable period of demoralization set into the anti-war movement, but it was remarkably brief. The resilience of peace activists, organizations, and coalitions in 2003–04 was a point of pride, and remains so today, as we have grown stronger despite understandable frustration with over four years of war. Peace Action remains an active member organization of UFPJ and of Win Without War.

In nearly all the cities and states where the nearly 100 affiliates and chapters of Peace Action are located, our activists are among the leaders in the local anti-war movement, mobilizing our members and concerned citizens, working in coalitions, pressuring Members of Congress, vigiling in local communities, organizing mass demonstrations, and sometimes engaging in non-violent civil disobedience.

In Washington, D.C., moving a supine Congress to oppose the occupation of Iraq more forcefully has been agonizingly, frustratingly slow. Paul Kawika Martin, our organizing and policy director, has been a tireless and effective advocate for Peace Action on Capitol Hill, both with key members of Congress and their staffs, as well as with colleague organizations, in developing legislative strategy. Peace Action, along with the Congressional Progressive Caucus, initiated the formation of the Iraq (and now also Iran) Coordinating Committee, a unique group drawing together peace organizations and Congressional staffers (and sometimes members of Congress) for meetings to share information and plan legislative strategy.

Although we will not be successful until all U.S. troops and bases are out of Iraq and the U.S. government commits to funding the rebuilding of that nation, we have made some significant progress in moving more members of Congress to speak out and take action in opposition to Bush's policies. The most noteworthy was the success in 2006 in securing the passage of federal legislation barring permanent U.S. military bases in Iraq, a seemingly small step that the Administration nonetheless fought tooth and nail.

Iran

The Bush administration's insistence on ratcheting up, instead of calming, tensions with Iran over its nuclear program adds a new challenge to the peace movement's already overflowing agenda. In early 2006,

Peace Action issued a statement authored by former New Jersey SANE Executive Director Herb Rothschild and Peace Action Education Fund board member Stephen Zunes calling for a renewed push to establish a Middle East Nuclear Weapons-Free Zone, which garnered both media attention and support among allies in the peace movement.

Peace Action staff helped play a catalyzing role in the spring and summer of 2006 in gathering movement and congressional allies together in several coalitions and working groups concerned with nuclear weapons and foreign policy issues to offer alternatives to Bush's obstinacy regarding Iran. Working groups on legislation and media communications regarding the Iran issue were formed, establishing better coordination among concerned peace and disarmament groups than previously existed. Unfortunately, US-Iran tensions over nuclear policy and other issues appear to provide a long-term challenge for peacemakers, in the United States and around the world. But they also present an opportunity to address larger issues of nuclear hypocrisy by nuclear-armed nations and regional security issues in the broader Middle East and Asia.

In addition to our policy and legislative work on the Iran issue, New Hampshire Peace Action Director Anne Miller and Peace Action of New York State Executive Director Melissa Van traveled to that nation in 2005 and 2006, respectively, on "citizen peacemaker" delegations. Upon returning, both Miller and Van gave dozens of public addresses and media interviews about their trips and their firm belief that the Iranian people want peace with the United States and with their neighbors in the region, despite the bellicose rhetoric of our two governments.

SPAN

The Student Peace Action Network (SPAN), a program of Peace Action Education Fund since 1996, now has contacts on about 100 college and university campuses, as well as high schools, across the United States. While SPAN has been vital to bringing thousands of young people into anti-war work, it has also provided seminal leadership to the burgeoning counter-military recruitment movement, as SPAN has grown from an almost entirely campus-based network to encompass broader community organizing. In counter-recruitment work, students and youth, parents, teachers, school administrators, veterans, and peace groups in the community team up to expose and oppose predatory military recruiting practices and offer positive educational and employment alternatives for young people who might otherwise consider the military as one of the best options for their future.

In 2005, Montclair, New Jersey, student and community activists, including New Jersey Peace Action staff and volunteers, joined together in their opposition to the military recruiting provision of the No Child Left Behind Act with a concerted effort to get opt-out forms and information distributed in the high school. A provision of the law states that schools must hand over student contact information to military recruiters or face losing their federal funding, unless the student or guardian opts out of having that information shared. Superb organizing and awareness-raising efforts resulted in over 91 percent of students opting-out of having their information shared with military recruiters. The activists didn't stop there; they took their concerns to the school board and demanded a district-wide policy change from opt-out to opt-in so that interested students would have to fill out a form requesting that their contact information be shared with military recruiters, a change that they were successful in creating. Today they continue to work toward changing the statewide policy to that of opting-in, though their efforts have thus far been rebuffed by the state school board.

Building Real Peace and Lasting Security through International Cooperation and Human Rights

Of course we have much to do at present to stop the Bush administration's assault on world peace, but we must also recognize the reality that the next president and Congress will spend most of their time and energy cleaning up Bush's political and fiscal mess.

We must see the "war on terror" and pre-emptive war doctrines for what they are—unsustainable, undemocratic schemes intended to intimidate the world and paralyze Americans with fear—and resoundingly reject them.

We in the peace movement will need to help teach the public and some policy makers, and possibly re-learn ourselves, what a responsible, diplomatically engaged U.S. foreign policy looks like.

Peace Action is well positioned to do exactly that, with our campaign—developed through grassroots and national-level organizing and affirmed in our Long-range Strategic Plan—for Real Security through International Cooperation and Human Rights. This simple message resonates with Americans because it reflects our values. Americans want to enhance international cooperation to address myriad problems—war, proliferation, the spread of AIDS, poverty, and global warming, to name but a few. We see it will be much more effective than our current government's unilateralist, go it alone, "do as we say not as we do" policies. Moreover it is the right thing to do. Upholding human rights is a keystone to enhancing global security, and is a value we hold dear, even when our government doesn't practice at home what it preaches abroad.

Also central is building a serious, even-handed commitment by our government to nuclear disarmament and non-proliferation. Without U.S. leadership to secure nuclear weapons technology and rid the earth of the scourge of nuclear weapons, nuclear proliferation and the global instability it breeds are practically guaranteed.

Unfortunately, the Bush administration is rewarding India's nuclear weapons program with a new deal to share nuclear material and technology; doing next to nothing about Pakistan's veritable nuclear Wal-Mart (because Pakistan's dictator, General Pervez Musharraf, is an "ally in the war on terror"); winking at Israel's nuclear arsenal; unilaterally dropping out of arms control treaties such as the Anti-Ballistic Missile Treaty; and ignoring our own obligations to pursue nuclear disarmament under the nuclear Non-Proliferation Treaty. There is no coherence to U.S. nuclear weapons policy, except, in the immortal words of George Herbert Walker Bush, "what we say goes."

His son George W. Bush may well go down in history as "the proliferation president." No president has ever been a better example of the adage: "When your only tool is a hammer, every problem looks like a nail."

Building Peace Action and Peace Action Education Fund in Order to Fulfill our Mission

Years ago, over dinner after a Peace Action organizers meeting, while discussing the state of the world, our movement, and our organization, a colleague stated: "We're not worthy of our dreams."

I was taken aback. At first I thought he meant we didn't deserve what we seek, but then he explained he meant we did not have the organizational and political capacity to transform or overcome the power of the war machine.

I still take this trenchant point to heart in my work, every day. Peace Action and the peace movement at large have the most wonderful, passionate, resilient, inspiring, doggedly determined people one could ever meet. They are our greatest strength. It is an honor and a blessing for me to get paid to work with such beautiful peace-mongers all over the country, and indeed with peace movement allies around the world.

However, if we are honest with ourselves, we must recognize that we have not succeeded in building a movement or an organization with the capacity to achieve our lofty goals.

We are not big enough, though we are growing. We are not politically powerful enough, though we are building that power. We are not diverse enough in terms of race, age, geographic reach, and political philosophy. How can we afford to exclude potential supporters and leaders?

As our board and staff leadership, along with consultants and legal counsel, looked at our Long-Range Strategic Plan, it became apparent that Peace Action Education Fund, the tax-deductible entity in the Peace Action family, was best suited to implement most of the objectives and functions prioritized in the plan.

So, after a small shift in 2006, in 2007 most of our programs and staff will migrate from Peace Action to Peace Action Education Fund (PAEF). As PAEF takes over from Peace Action the role of "senior partner," almost nobody inside or outside the organization will notice the difference in our work. (Many of our colleague organizations have been structured this way for years.)

Specifically, this restructuring will enable us to develop and invest more resources in our organization's growth, in our organizing, program, and legislative work, and in supporting our network of chapters and affiliates in nearly 30 states around the country, which are Peace Action's unique strength.

PAEF will also be making significant investments in on-line advocacy and fundraising, new donor growth, and enhancement of our major donor and planned-giving programs. These investments will increase available resources for our non-partisan Peace Voter and presidential candidate bird-dogging efforts in 2007–08, and also our ongoing media, legislative, and political work. And we will continue to play the strong leadership or catalyst role we play in various coalitions in the peace movement, and with our grassroots affiliate and chapter network.

Our organization's structure may have served us well in the years since the SANE/Freeze merger, but it is clear that is no longer the case. As we enter middle age (we are in our fifties, after all!), we must re-think how we can best build our organization and our political power to further the struggle for a peaceful world.

Chapter 14

Real Security in the Future: International Cooperation, Human Rights, and Freedom from Weapons of Mass Destruction

Steven Brion-Meisels and Glen Harold Stassen

Three strategies dominate current U.S. foreign policy, and they have tragic implications for the future. *Unilateral domination,* rather than international cooperation, along with increasing *militarism,* are at the heart of the problem, and they have led to a disregard for economic and political *human rights* at home and abroad. Peace Action's roots, history, and strategies offer a powerful alternative for our nation's leaders and citizens. In this chapter, we look back to learn from what has empowered our movement. We look forward to the years that lie ahead. We articulate Peace

Action's comprehensive plan for Real Security—based on international cooperation, freedom from weapons of mass destruction, and the primacy of human rights at home and abroad. We advocate some concrete peace actions that can initiate a steady move toward real security—and avoid the catastrophes that lie ahead on our nation's current road. And we show how the actions work together for Real Security through International Cooperation and Human Rights.

Fifty Years in the Future: Two Snapshots

The violence of September 11, 2001, offered our nation a unique if painful opportunity to change the direction of our foreign policy. After our mourning and shock, two doors faced us. Our government chose the door of fear and domination—which led to unilateralism, militarism, and an increasing disregard for human rights.

Fortress America

If current trends continue, our nation will be an ever-more isolated, fearful, and dangerous fortress in an unending and unlimited "War Against Terrorism" that increases the amount of hatred and the number of terrorist attacks against the United States and other lands. Concrete and legal walls will keep out all but the smallest percentage of immigrants. Demand for fossil fuel, combined with shrinking supply, will create a desperate impulse to seize oil from wilderness, ocean, and other nations. The search for bio-fuel replacements will shrink the planet's already diminished water supply.[1] Fueled by fear, militarism, and economic decline, our growing national debt will either bankrupt our economy or make us indentured servants to international bankers. Scarcity and fear will erode the fundamental democratic processes that have defined our vision of America. Headlines tell us these trends have already begun; even more dire implications lie unspoken or still cloaked in state secrecy. We have a moral responsibility to avoid this future—for our children and for our planet.

Real Security and Community

The second door still beckons, unopened. It leads to the opposite of all that we describe above. International cooperation and treaties for freedom from weapons of mass destruction, with the U.S. sharing responsibilities along with other nations, will free up billions of dollars for real security at home and abroad. With funds rescued from our bloated military budget, our nation can repair and upgrade civilian infrastructure and ensure affordable housing, health care, and education for our citizens; abolish the threat of nuclear weapons; and reduce if not eradicate global poverty—with consequent benefits for increased environmental health and reduced population growth. There will be no need to "export democracy" by force, as our current foreign policy is alleged to do. We will spread democracy by cooperating with global civic and faith-based movements to spread human rights. This process has worked dramatically in Latin America, where autocracy used to reign in most countries and democracy is now emerging—without the U.S. government using military force to spread it. Our nation will regain a positive place in the world community.

We will experience an internal change inside our own self-awarenesses from fear to cooperation. Knowing that the rest of the world will see the United States less as a go-it-alone bully than it now does, and more as a cooperative support alongside the UN and others to nudge nations toward human rights and justice, we will have a clearer sense of ourselves as cooperators rather than aggressors. We will see terrorists as criminals to be dealt with justly and potential terrorists as human beings who can be shown a better way to pursue justice. Shifting from fear to cooperation, we will have less unconscious need to see others as an angry potential threat and more hope and gratitude for what cooperation does occur. We will begin to breathe a sigh of relief from the hostile feelings of the past few years. Our children and our neighbors around the planet will thank us.

A Brief Look Back

When Peace Action was born in 1957 as the Committee for a Sane Nuclear Policy, our political focus was on disarmament—in response to the grave threats that resulted from nuclear testing and nuclear saber rattling. However, our founders understood the connections among disarmament, international cooperation, and human rights.

Militarism has cost countless lives at home and abroad, broken our formerly healthy national budget, accelerated environmental degradation, destroyed much of our social infrastructure, made us the world's leading exporter of weapons, seduced us into breaking or ignoring international treaties, and caused much of the world to look at the U.S. government with dismay.

A *neglect of human rights* at home and abroad has caused us to incarcerate millions of young men and women (mostly poor and with dark skin) with a billion-dollar-plus annual price tag, allow New Orleans to drown beneath Katrina's waves, maintain a two-tier system of education and employment, support death squads and repression abroad, dump toxic military and technological waste outside our borders, export cigarettes and weapons rather than medical aid, ignore or under-represent the impact of global poverty on people of color, waste oil to feed over-sized automobiles, and enforce "Free Trade" rather than Fair Trade relationships with other nations.

Unilateral foreign policy strategies have caused us to abrogate critical disarmament and environmental treaties, threaten and bully the United Nations, ignore our historic allies, proclaim an Axis of Evil and an unending War on Terror, export weapons that cause civilians to suffer needlessly, alienate the world's second largest religion (Islam), and find ourselves left to clean up a tragic human and economic mess left by the war on Iraq. The administration of George W. Bush has blocked or withdrawn from critical treaties, including those providing for a comprehensive nuclear test ban, a halt to fissile materials, chemical weapons, and biological weapons production, a ban on antiballistic missiles and land mines, implementation of the Kyoto Accords to halt global warming, and establishment of an International Criminal Court. Almost every other nation has ratified these treaties, but the U.S. has stood alone against them—as if not caring about the spread of weapons of mass destruction, the preservation of the environment, and the protection of human rights.

Learning from Our Past: The Strength of a Unifying Strategy

One clear lesson from this book is that we gained enormous strength and influence when we adopted a unifying strategy—both in the early efforts of SANE and in the later work of the Freeze Campaign. Membership in our grassroots organizations multiplied a hundredfold, and we won support in the polls from 72 percent of the American people. We secured congressional budget changes that blocked the MX missile, anti-satellite missiles, antiballistic missiles, weapons that violated the

SALT II Treaty, and other weapons the Reagan administration wanted. In accordance with the Freeze bilateral strategy, we got Congress to halt the funding so long as the Soviet Union also avoided funding the same developments—and the Soviet Union reciprocated. Pressures from the Freeze were a major force behind the elimination of all medium-range nuclear missiles in Europe, sizable reductions in stockpiles of other nuclear weapons, and an end to the Cold War.

What can we learn from the Freeze Campaign's growing strength in the 1980s? We had a unified strategy, instead of scattered campaigns to oppose specific weapons. We had a single clear and positive theme: the demand for a bilateral halt in development, testing, and deployment of all nuclear weapons. We had a framing narrative that clearly diagnosed the error that people saw was causing their fear—the escalating nuclear arms race—and that clearly described the way out—a bilateral halt. Our narrative was readily understood—stop the nuclear arms race. It did not require elite, recondite knowledge of what each missile and bomber was and what special dangers or imbalances each one threatened. It could and did convert "middle America" and win the support of the large majority of Americans. It demanded a radical change: halt all nuclear weapons. But it incorporated the conservative sensibility that the Soviet Union needed to halt too, and that its halt needed to be verifiable. "Don't trust the Russians; trust our satellites, seismographs, and on-site inspections." And it would make a big difference for issues we cared about: greater safety for our children, reduction in the nuclear threat, saving billions of dollars, moving toward peace. It connected with parents' concern for their children.

Peace Action now has a unifying campaign that can give us strength to make a major difference for the issues we care about. The campaign doesn't look as simple as just halting the nuclear arms race. But it didn't look so simple back then, either.

Our unifying strategy is *Real Security through International Cooperation and Human Rights*. It gives specificity to our previous Campaign for a New Foreign Policy, and it incorporates strengths of the SMART Security program of Physicians for Social Responsibility. Its framing narrative clearly diagnoses the problem: reliance on making wars by go-it-alone unilateralism. Our alternative can be readily understood: start cooperating with the treaties that stop the spread of weapons of mass destruction and prevent torture of defenseless prisoners; work with other nations and the United Nations whose cooperation we need in order to prevent recruitment to terrorism and wars against countries like Iraq,

Iran, and North Korea. It can win the support of Middle America and large majorities of U.S. citizens. On the one hand, it is conservative: Americans want us to be law-abiding citizens in the world, and we want the respect of other nations. On the other hand, it makes a radical difference: we prevent further unilateral "preemptive" interventionist wars, and we work toward Senate ratification of the treaties that stop the spread of weapons of mass destruction.

And it will make a big difference for goals we care about: greater safety for our children, reduction of the nuclear threat, saving billions of dollars, and sustainable peace with justice.

The World Turns toward Connection:
Connect with Reality

The world is turning toward connection and interdependence in economic, health, environmental, social, and political ways. As with most drastic changes, these shifts offer both peril and promise. But they show that policies of unilateralist isolation are out of touch with reality. The reality is our increasing interconnectedness.

International NGOs are increasing rapidly and are connecting us together more and more. Corporate globalization has intensified the fragile interdependence of our planet and its peoples. Potentially catastrophic environmental changes will soon knit the lifestyles of all of us together—the wealthy few as well as the many whom Archbishop Oscar Romero called "los empobridos"—the impoverished. Multinational corporations move resources beyond the reach of government oversight while creating a global trap for low-wage and marginalized workers. But they also connect nations together and give the lie to policies of unilateralism. Even terrorist networks have now become international and can be countered adequately only by international cooperation. As Stanley Hoffman writes, "There is now a transnational society that includes multinational corporations, non-governmental organizations, criminals, and terrorists."[2]

At the same time, the growth of international cooperation offers promise for peacemaking and real security. The communications revolution spreads democracy and new ideas. The environmental threat calls all of us to cooperative action, and our increased understanding of environmental connectedness provides new strategies. Human migration leads to new patterns of intercultural understanding that will shift religious, cultural, and even family patterns. Economic interaction has created new alliances across cultures, borders, social class, gender, and generation. The growth of non-governmental environmental, peace, and human rights organizations continue to make real international cooperation a reality—while offering support for strengthening international organizations like the United Nations and the World Court. Throughout human evolution, the most effective response to threat has been not fight or flight, but cooperation in support of shared security.

Framing Our Work within a Unifying Narrative

Our comprehensive campaign for Real Security through International Cooperation and Human Rights requires us to frame all our specific campaigns in the same unified narrative, so that narrative captures the imagination of the people. When the people frame their understanding of specific threats and policies in this narrative, we win.

George Lakoff is an expert on how people process information. His widely read book *Don't Think of an Elephant* says the key to mobilizing people for progressive goals like cooperation, disarmament, and human rights is NOT bombarding them with facts or isolated issue campaigns. Rather, the goal is to help people to think and act within a new narrative—one that provides a unifying approach to progressive social change. That's what our long-range strategy program seeks to help all of us do.

Our narrative is simple and compelling: unilateralist, go-it-alone policies that rely on U.S. military domination and disrespect for human rights have caused international anger at the United States, more recruits to terrorism, one disaster after another, and a much less secure world. Now we, the people, are rising up to correct this: We need and we demand real security through international cooperation and human rights.

Our Analysis: Unilateralism, Militarism, and Human Rights

Why is there terrorism? Why do terrorists hate us so much? These questions have haunted many Americans since September 11, 2001. One answer has become clear: our nation's unilateral policies of warmaking and violation of human rights of Arabs and Muslims.

Why have Iran and North Korea apparently begun to develop nuclear weapons? Because the U.S. government abandoned the international cooperation policies (treaties, diplomacy, and economic pressure) that persuaded Brazil, Argentina, Libya, and South Africa to reverse their efforts to develop nuclear weapons. Instead the Bush administration—labeling Iraq, Iran, and North Korea "the axis of evil"—threatened them with war, refused their request for a treaty of nonaggression, and refused to talk with them. After the U.S. military conquest of Iraq, Iran and North Korea apparently decided they'd better have a deterrent against U.S. attack.

Why did some U.S. soldiers torture prisoners? Because the administration abandoned the protection of international law for prisoners (the Geneva Convention) and instead defended torture.

Why did the U.S. government undermine six different treaties that work to prevent the spread of nuclear, chemical, and biological weapons? Because the Bush administration opposes treaties and abiding by international law and instead relies on U.S. military weapons.

Why is the U.S. spending itself into bankruptcy for enormous increases in weapons and war making? Because of go-it-alone reliance on U.S. military power and abandonment of international cooperation and respect for the United Nations and human rights.

Why did the United States put itself in a position where thousands of lives and large parts of an ancient culture have been lost in Iraq? Our government arrogantly made the war as a go-it-alone action while ignoring the checks and balances of the United Nations and other nations, the reports of international inspectors that no weapons could be found, and the warnings of the international Red Cross that torture and abuse were taking place.

Blazoned across the cover of *Time* magazine for July 17, 2006, was "The End of Cowboy Diplomacy: What North Korea, Iraq, and Iran Teach Us About the Limits of Going It Alone." The cover article says: "'It's difficult to think of many other times and many other presidencies when so many dangerous events were happening at once. . . . The biggest illusion of the Bush doctrine was the idea that that U.S. could carry out a strategy as ambitious as reshaping the Middle East . . . without a degree of international legitimacy and cooperation to back it up."

Our government's unilateral policies undermine our real security. The United States can contribute to world peace and security much more effectively by working in tandem with international networks and treaties for human rights and freedom from weapons of mass destruction.

International Cooperation, Freedom from Weapons of Mass Destruction, and Support for Human Rights

Much of what has been wrong and destructive about recent U.S. foreign policy can be diagnosed and articulated within a single narrative: the need for international cooperation, weapons-reduction, and support for human rights. The same narrative frames the goals that Peace Action has adopted for real security.

International Cooperation instead of Unilateralism

The genius of the U.S. Constitution is the separation of powers: each branch of government checks and balances the power of other branches, as the Supreme Court checked and balanced the administration's plans for kangaroo courts to try people imprisoned in Guantanamo. The wisdom in this procedure lies in the fact that concentrating power in one power-center without checks and balances leads to tyranny and injustice. The U.S. has an enormous concentration of military and economic power. We need the checks and balances of respect for international cooperation and international support for human rights, or else the U.S. government drifts toward empire and injustice.

The struggle against terrorism can be far more effective if the U.S. works in cooperation with, not against, other nations. Here are some concrete directions Peace Action's unifying strategy sets forth for a comprehensive program that supports international cooperation:

- Work to end the U.S. policies that support "pre-emptive war." Emphasize global cooperation as a wiser and more effective path toward real security.
- Secure Senate ratification of international treaties that support real security by controlling or eliminating testing and production of nuclear, biological, and chemical weapons, landmines, and weapons in space.
- Expand and sustain U.S. funding for multinational peacekeeping forces trained and equipped to prevent armed conflict or to respond rapidly to conflict.

Peace Action selects one or two of our objectives at a time for our major push. And we get results. Recently in tandem with others, we focused on convincing the nation that war in Iraq and war against Iran were foolish and wrong. Awareness of failures of go-it-alone policies has brought the nation to a "teachable moment," when we can learn the wrongness of such wars and the rightness of shifting toward international cooperation.

People know that unilateral and militaristic policies have cost the United States enormously in international reputation. The Gallup Poll in June 9–11, 2006, asked Americans if "the image of the U.S. around the world" was better off, the same, or worse off because of the Iraq War. Strikingly, 60 percent believed the international image of the U.S. was worse off, and only 11 percent thought it was better off.

Freedom from Weapons of Mass Destruction instead of Militarism

Real security can be achieved through the long-range objectives Peace Action has adopted for freedom from weapons of mass destruction. Here are some concrete examples:

- Block funding for the production and testing of new nuclear weapons. In recent years, we focused on preventing appropriations for the nuclear "bunker buster"—a weapon designed for first use. In tandem with others, we succeeded.
- Expand and sustain U.S. contributions to international programs designed to secure, reduce, and eliminate existing nuclear stockpiles that degrade the environment and are a threat in the hands of governments or terrorists. This goal is within reach; it has political support.
- Secure ratification of international treaties that control or eliminate weapons of mass destruction. This requires learning that international cooperation is more effective than going it alone.
- Reduce the U.S. military budget, including production of conventional weapons and the sale or export of weapons abroad.

Respect for Human Rights

Real security is linked inextricably with human rights. Career diplomat John Brady Kiesling left his position in the State Department because he could no longer accept his government's policies for war in Iraq. He argues that "morality and self-interest are inseparable, provided we persuade our politicians to take a long enough view of these interests. In the long run, security cannot be purchased at the expense of justice."[3]

Real Security is enhanced by the protection of economic and political rights. Scholars remind us that democracies with human rights do not make war against each other, especially when they are linked by economic and political incentives to cooperate—as the post-World-War-II success of Europe and Japan attest.[4] Poverty in places like Gaza, and oppressive regimes in nations like Saudi Arabia, Pakistan, and Egypt, provide fertile ground for terrorist recruitment—especially when those conditions are exacerbated by U.S. weapons sales and military aid.

Peace Action's objectives can reduce the hatred that causes terrorism. Here are some concrete actions we advocate:

- Redirect U.S. military expenditures toward human rights needs at home and abroad—including health care, education, renewable energy, and environmental clean-up and protection.
- Restrict and reduce the international weapons trade: ban the sale of U.S. weapons to governments that violate human rights, and redirect funds to provide peacekeeping and reconstruction in areas that have been ravaged by human rights violations.
- Strengthen international programs that work for human rights and social justice—including programs for fair trade, sustainable development, civilian-led democratization, peaceful conflict resolution, and reduction of world poverty.

Peace Action is confident that these measures will enhance our national security. If we acquiesce to the policy of unilateral domination, our lives can only become more anxious and our future more grim. If, instead, we choose human rights, international cooperation, and freedom from weapons of mass destruction, real security will be our reward.

Real Security: A Unified Plan and Integrated Actions

We have a clearly focused long-range plan for Peace Action: Real Security through International Cooperation and Human Rights. *Real* security does not mean lavishing our resources on more military build-ups. It means reducing the threat from weapons of mass destruction and terrorism; and decreasing recruitment to terrorism by working for the human rights of all rather than by attacking and occupying other people's homelands. Real security means safe and sustainable jobs, good schools, affordable health care, and renewable energy. Real security builds cooperation with other nations and peoples of the world so we all work together against preemptive wars and terrorism.[5]

Our concrete actions will be more effective as they are integrated into a comprehensive framework. We believe that this kind of integration—in our vision, our diagnosis of what's wrong, our language, and our actions—is the key to a sustained program for real security in the years ahead. We believe that the future of Peace Action must be built on this kind of integrated approach, and that these integrated peace actions will help us realize a future worthy of our children. Our friend and former Peace Action President, William Sloane Coffin Jr., wrote: "Hope is a passion for the possible, a determination that our children not be asked to shoulder burdens that we let fall. Hopeful people are always critical of the present but only because they hold such a bright view of the future."[6]

Notes

1. For more on these connections, see Lester Brown's *Plan B.2A: Rescuing a Planet in Stress and a Civilization in Trouble* (New York: W.W. Norton, 2006).

2. *New York Review of Books* (August 10, 2006), 60.

3. John Brady Kiesling, *Diplomacy Lessons: Realism for an Unloved Superpower* (Washington, D.C.: Potomac Books, 2006).

4. Glen Stassen, ed., *Just Peacemaking: Ten Practices for Abolishing War* (Cleveland: Pilgrim Press: 1998 and 2004), chapters 5 and 6.

5. For more on real security, see Richard Barnet's classic work, *Real Security* (New York: Simon and Schuster, 1981).

6. *A Passion for the Possible* (Louisville: Westminster John Knox Press, 1993), 3.

Index

About the Contributors

The Rev. Dr. **Andrea Ayvazian** is pastor of the Haydenville Congregational Church in Western Massachusetts. The former Dean of Religious Life at Mount Holyoke College, Andrea is an anti-racism educator and war tax resister. She was director of training at the Peace Development Fund in the 1980s, and part of the team that forged the merger of SANE and the Freeze.

Steven Brion-Meisels has been active in peace and justice work for 35 years. He has worked in schools and communities, has served on the National Board of Peace Action, and has worked to link local and international peacemaking through his teaching and writing. His wife and two daughters inspire and support what Bill Coffin called "a passion for the possible."

David Cortright is a research fellow at the Joan B. Kroc Institute for International Peace Studies at the University of Notre Dame and president of the Fourth Freedom Forum. He was executive director of SANE from 1977 to 1987 and is the author or co-editor of fourteen books, including *Peace Works: The Citizen's Role in Ending the Cold War* (Boulder, CO: Westview Press, 1993).

Sanford Gottlieb joined SANE in 1957 and served, successively, as volunteer chair of the Washington chapter and as political action director (1960–67) and executive director (1967–77) of National SANE. After leaving SANE, he was executive director of two other arms control organizations and producer of the Center for Defense Information's weekly TV program. He is the author of *Defense Addiction*.

Monica Green, president of Peace Action Education Fund, lives in Northampton, Massachusetts, with her husband, Rich West, and their three children. Green was executive director of the Greater Cleveland Freeze from 1985 to 1989, co-chaired the SANE/Freeze merger transition team, moved to Washington, D.C., in 1989 to be national field director, then served as national executive director of Peace Action from 1991 to 1995.

Homer A. Jack, a Unitarian-Universalist minister, was a long-time activist in movements for peace and racial equality. A founder of SANE, he served as its executive director from 1960 to 1964. Thereafter, he worked as director of the Division of Social Responsibility of the Unitarian Universalist Association (1964–70) and as secretary general of the World Conference on Religion and Peace (1970–83). He died in 1995.

Randy Kehler was National Coordinator of the Freeze Campaign from 1981 to 1984. During the Vietnam War, he worked in the West Coast office of the War Resisters League and was imprisoned as a conscientious draft-resister. With Ben Senturia, he organized the Working Group on Election Democracy for full public funding of elections. His current project—Promoting Active Nonviolence—deals with youth.

Barbara Lee was elected to represent California's Ninth Congressional district in 1998. The co-chair of the Congressional Progressive Caucus, she serves on the House International Relations Committee. She has been a leader in promoting policies to foster international peace, security, and human rights, and has sponsored legislation to disavow the doctrine of preventive war and to create a cabinet-level Department of Peace.

Kevin Martin has served as executive director of Peace Action and Peace Action Education Fund since September 2001. He has worked with the organization in various capacities, including door-to-door canvasser and executive director of Illinois Peace Action in Chicago, since 1985. He lives in Silver Spring, Maryland, with his wife, fellow peace activist Susan Udry, and their children, Maya and Max.

Patricia McCullough, Ph.D., is a clinical psychologist working with children in Cleveland. She has an M.A. in Political Science specializing in national security issues. She was director of the Council on Peacemaking and Religion in Louisville from 1980 to 1990, and served as co-chair of the Executive Committee of the Freeze Campaign. She is the mother of four children, grandmother of one, and cares about their future—without war.

Ria Pugeda is a Senior Program Associate at the Public Welfare Foundation. She worked at the Eastern Office of the Tides Foundation and Tides Center as coordinator and project services associate respectively. Ria was the administrator of the International Program of SANE/Freeze: Campaign for Global Security. She also served as the administrative officer of the Philippine Resource Center.

Marcus Raskin was co-founder of the Institute for Policy Studies, as well as a co-chair of SANE. He is a professor in the Graduate Public Policy Program at George Washington University, a member of the *Nation* editorial board, and an author/editor of books on political theory, international relations, and government. His most recent book is *The Four Freedoms Under Siege*.

Jim Rice is editor of *Sojourners* magazine. Before coming to Sojourners in 1982, Rice was an organizer for the Center for Peace Studies at Georgetown University. He was founder of Pax Christi: Washington's Peace Education Program, served on the founding National Committee and Executive Committee of the Nuclear Weapons Freeze Campaign, and was treasurer of the Nuclear Weapons Education Fund.

Ben Senturia was referendum coordinator and political education coordinator for the national staff of the Nuclear Weapons Freeze Campaign, and then a board member of SANE/Freeze. He provides capacity-building consulting and training for social change groups. He is also board chair of Missouri Votes Conservation, vice president of ALL God's People, and co-facilitator of the Democracy Committee of the Threshold Foundation.

Glen Harold Stassen, Smedes Professor of Christian Ethics, Fuller Theological Seminary, edited *Just Peacemaking: Ten Practices for Abolishing*

War, and authored *Just Peacemaking: Transforming Initiatives for Peace and Justice, Living the Sermon on the Mount,* and *Kingdom Ethics.* He served on the International Committee, co-chaired the Strategy Committee, and chaired the Euromissile Committee of the Freeze Campaign; and is a board member of Peace Action.

Jim Wallis is a bestselling author (*God's Politics: Why the Right Gets It Wrong and the Left Doesn't Get It*), public theologian, speaker, and international commentator on ethics and public life. He is president of Sojourners/Call to Renewal, where he is editor-in-chief of *Sojourners* magazine and convenes a national network of churches, faith-based organizations, and individuals working to overcome poverty in America.

Cora Weiss, who launched the idea of an International Office and International Committee for SANE/Freeze, has devoted her life to movements for civil rights, human rights, women's rights, and peace. She has served as president of the International Peace Bureau and of the Hague Appeal for Peace, which issued the Hague Agenda for Peace and Justice for the 21st Century: www.haguepeace.org.

Lawrence Wittner, professor of history at the State University of New York/Albany, has written or edited numerous books on peace and foreign policy issues, including the award-winning trilogy, *The Struggle Against the Bomb.* A former president of the Peace History Society, he has been active for decades in peace, racial equality, and labor organizations. He is currently a National Board member of Peace Action.